SECRET SITES OF HISTORIC TRIVIA IN SAN DIEGO

Secret Sites of Historic Trivia in San Diego

by
William Carroll

First Edition

Printed in the United States of America
ISBN 0-910390-39-8
Library of Congress Catalog Number 94-94297

Coda Publications
P.O. Bin 711
San Marcos, California 92079-0711, U.S.A.

For the explorer in all of us.

Contents

The Cab Drivers' Fountain near Horton Plaza.

The beautiful cover photograph, of Villa Montezuma (1887) which is described on Page 85, was provided by the San Diego Historical Society.

About This Book

San Diego has its share of the odd and unusual and in this book you'll find over 225 of the best. Many are just around the corner. A few may call for a day's drive but with planning and a map book you may be able to visit a goodly number of ***Secret Sites*** during one outing. However, be not surprised if something has changed, been moved or no longer exists. All were photographed prior to publication but "progress" being the monster that it is it's possible some of our best may be missing in the future.

Beginning on the next page the ***Sites*** are sequenced in alphabetic order by their location or community name. For example, when you look up Harborside you will find a number of ***Secret Sites*** in that location. The complete Index is fairly long because ***Sites*** are cross-indexed by name and again by location.

Individual listings include one or more photographs, a street address and the ***Thomas Guide San Diego County Street Directory*** page and grid number locators. In 1993 ***Thomas Guide*** page numbers were revised and the new locators are used in this book. The map coordinates in this book do not apply to ***Guides*** published prior to 1993. A description of each ***Site*** is included to assist in determining those you would like most to visit. When available, you will find the ***Site's*** telephone number to call for additional information.

A few ***Sites*** are public attraction features which sometimes modify their hours or cost of admission to meet current needs. For these it may be worthwhile to telephone ahead for an update on the current policy. Thought not really ***Secret*** the many attractions of Balboa Park make it worthwhile to visit the Information Office on the Prado. It offers a "Museum Passport" which provides inexpensive entry to the Park's fine exhibits. It is an exceptional value as is the dual-use Zoological ticket for entry to both the world-renowned San Diego Zoo and the Wild Animal Park.

Be all that as it may, have fun exploring a bit more of San Diego and its wonderful background of historic trivia.

Anza-Borrego

Agua Caliente Hot Springs

39555 County Highway S-2, Julian 92036
Information Sources: 595-3600

Thomas Guide Pg.430, D/3

At the foot of the Tierra Blanca mountains of Anza-Borrego State Park is San Diego County's Agua Caliente Hot Springs Park.

This public park has a large outdoor warm swimming pool, an indoor spa where the water is decidedly hot and a modest cold-water outdoor pool filled from a nearby spring. There is room for camping and RV parking. A major feature of the Hot Springs is several nearby hiking trails for the active. It is possible to inspect the remains of crude ponds constructed many years ago by Indians living in the area. Telephone first as the facility may not be open during the hot months of June through September.

Solar heating brings temperature of this indoor pool to spa warmth. Dressing rooms are on the left under the Quonset roof, the pool area is to the right under the solar panel array. Pool use is included in the park admission charge for camping or RV parking with full or partial hook-ups. A food store is nearby.

Anza-Borrego

Anza Campsites (1774-1775)

El Vado and Los Puertecitos, Anza-Borrego State Pk 92004
Information Sources: 767-4684 *Thomas Guide Pg.Noted*

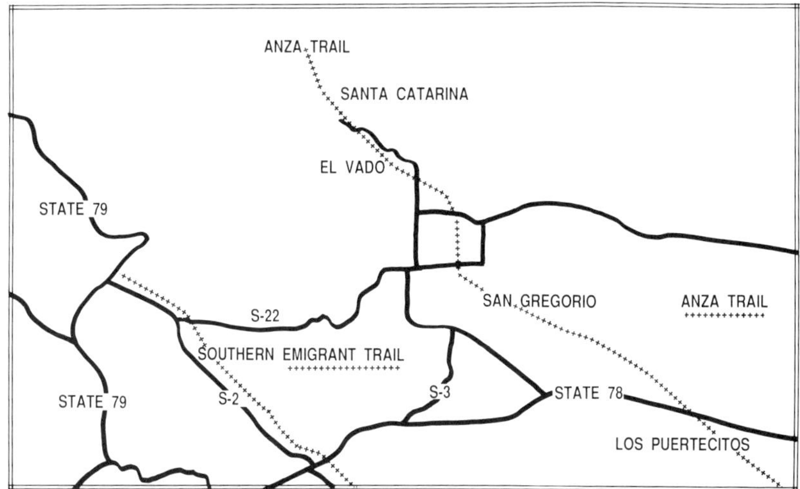

El Vado is where the same 240 Spanish soldiers and immigrants from Sonora, Mexico, camped December 20-22 in 1775. It is located east off Borrego Springs Road (*Pg. 410, B/5*) on a dirt road not often suitable for cars.

Anza-Borrego

Emigrant Wagon Pass (1847)

On County S-2 South of Highway 78, Shelter Valley 92036
Information Sources: 767-4684 *Thomas Guide Pg.430, B/1*

It was in this rugged land that members of the Mormon Battalion chipped away solid rock from a narrow gorge around a corner on the right to allow the axles of their wagons to pass through on January 19, 1847. By standing near the monument overlooking Box Canyon it is possible to see the Mormon's trail as the narrow upper path on the opposite hillside. The lower and wider roadway on the same hillside was used by the Butterfield Stages of 1858. Both of these are only a few feet above the dry river bed which is wider than either historic trail.

These paths were part of the Southern Emigrant Trail which was one of the few all-weather routes into California. This Box Canyon passage was also used by wagon trains and for a while by the U.S.Army's short-lived Camel Corps.

Anza-Borrego

Foot and Walker Pass (1847)

County S-2, Blair Valley, Anza-Borrego Park 92004
Information Sources: 767-4684 *Thomas Guide Pg.430, B/2*

This easily reached site along the Southern Emigrant Trail has a history of intensive use including the Mormon Battalion during its march to San Diego and Butterfield Stages on their runs between Tipton, Missouri, and San Francisco.

The Blair Valley turnoff is adjacent to Post Mile marker 23 on County Highway S-2. Although the signed entry road is rough it is usable by passenger cars. Within a half mile there is a parking area on the left at the base of the Pass. A descriptive historical monument is hidden on the right about halfway up the slope.

The steep pass is over solid rock which was much too smooth for stage horses to hold their footing though wheel ruts of the stages can be found. When the stage was heavy with express, passengers had to disembark at the base of the pass and walk or push the stage up the slope before being allowed to reboard and continue their journey: Therefore the name *Foot and Walker Pass.* The Butterfield run from Tipton to San Francisco involved 24 days of travel over 2000 miles of rough country and often unfriendly native Americans. During the Civil War U.S. soldiers were stationed along the route to guard stages and passengers.

The route of the Mormon Battalion continued northward as they worked their way toward San Diego. The Battalion was formed in 1846 to assist in the nation's war with Mexico. 500 Men and nearly 80 women and children left western Iowa on July 16, 1846. Their more than 2000-mile trek is recorded as the longest infantry march in U.S. military history.

The Mormons arrived in San Diego on January 29, 1847. They occupied what is now known as Fort Stockton in Presidio Park and are credited with being instrumental in bringing the war with Mexico to a close. As time permitted members of the group dug wells, created pumps to draw water and erected the first brick kiln in California in addition to establishing the first bakery and blacksmith shop. During this period, in April of the same year, one of the women gave birth to a son. Later the Battalion was transferred to Los Angeles. A few discharged soldiers went north to build a sawmill for John Sutter and soon became involved with searching for gold following Sutter's discovery.

Anza-Borrego

Jackass Mail (1857)

On County S-2, One Mile North of 78, Scissors Crossing 92036
Information Sources: 767-4684 *Thomas Guide Pg.410, A/11*

This is a site marker for the nation's first transcontinental mail service. It began on July 9, 1857 when driver James Mason left San Antonio, Texas, for San Diego. Mail and passengers arrived 53 days later after 1500 miles of crosscounty travel.

As described then, "Passengers and express matter (are) forwarded in new coaches drawn by six mules over the entire length of (the) line, excepting for the Colorado (Anza-Borrego) Desert of 100 miles which (are) crossed on mule back." Accordingly the line was known as the "Jackass Mail." Butterfield Stages, the Civil War and Indian attacks closed the service within two years.

Anza-Borrego

Palm Canyon

State Park Access Road, Anza-Borrego Park 92004
Information Sources: 767-4684 *Thomas Guide Pg.1058, E/7*

This is the trail head to one of the most interesting walks in the Anza-Borrego Desert State Park. It's about a mile and a half to the palm grove up a gentle slope which rises about 350 feet. The canyon walk is ripe with bird life and tiny desert animals. The palm stand has a constant supply of water from mountain springs and in past years was home to native Americans who made good use of its natural shelters. Pottery shards and bedrock morteros, for grinding nuts and seeds, have been found as artifacts of centuries of habitation. As you hike upward you will pass over an alluvial fan, through groves of ocotillo and along a dry wash which in the winter is a flowing stream. Layered rocks on adjacent cliffs represent some of the oldest rocks in the Park. An excellent map-guide is available at no charge.

Anza-Borrego Southern Emigrant Trail (1840-1850)

County Highway S-2, Anza-Borrego Park 92004
Information Sources: 767-4684 *Thomas Guide Pg.1158, F/4*

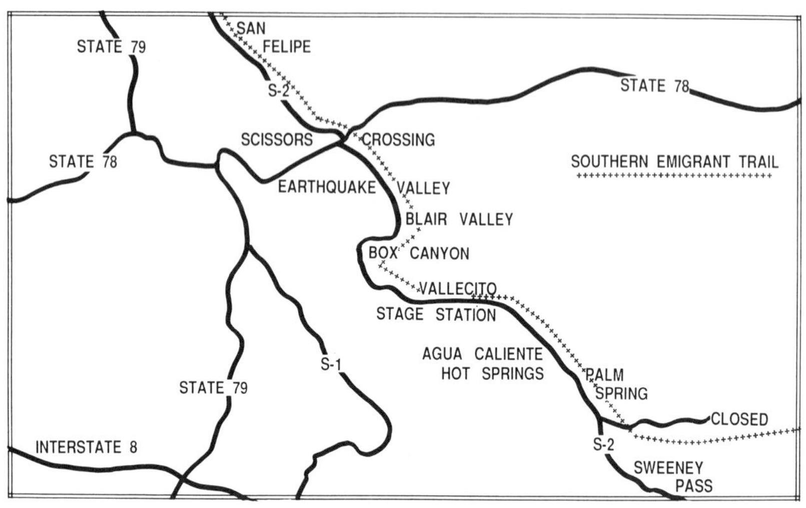

Historic stage roads and explorer trails abound in the Anza-Borrego Desert State Park with the caveat that exploration is best enjoyed from November to April. This trip from Highway 78 south on County S-2 will take from two to three hours for the 25-mile tour and its many frequent points of interest.

Much of the alignment of County Highway S-2 is the Southern Emigrant Trail Historic Route which was used by Butterfield Stages, The Mormon Battalion, the famous "Jackass Mail" and thousands of emigrants on their way into California. Obtain a brochure, map and guidance from Park Headquarters which also stocks books on explorer and pioneer travelers crossing the desert.

Spanish explorers passed through the area. Later Kit Carson, and the Mormon Battalion, followed the same route. During the 1840 to 1850 period this was one of the very few year-around wagon roads usable for emigrants from eastern states. There's much to see along this brief section of County S-2 and it all merits time and exploration to savor the romance of the historic route.

The portion from Highway 78 north and south includes site of the San Felipe Stage Station, Foot and Walker Pass, Box Canyon, the reconstructed Vallecito Stage Station and Palm Spring where in 1782 Pedro Fages recorded the first palms found in California. In 1858 this site was a watering stop between the Carrizo and Vallecito stage stations. (See Index for additional information.)

Anza-Borrego

Southern Overland Stage Route 1849

Highway S-2 at Sweeney Pass Road, Anza-Borrego Desert 92004
Information Sources: 767-4684 *Thomas Guide Pg.430, E/4*

Near Sweeney Pass the original unpaved stage road in the background merges with the pavement of County S-2 to continue northward as a portion of the southern stage route to San Francisco. A few miles north is the Vallecito Butterfield Stage Station (*430, C/2*) where tired horses and passengers were refreshed.

At the junction of what is now State Highway 79 and S-2, there was a wagon road which led southward into San Diego. However the stage route continued north past Warner Ranch to the next Butterfield station at Oak Grove (409, H/5) and then on to Temecula over a route similar to State Highway 79.

Anza-Borrego

Wildflowers

P.O.Box 299, Borrego Springs 92004
Information Sources: 767-4684 *Thomas Guide Pg.1078, B/3*

When the desert lights up with the colorful blooms of its normally hidden flowers, the most effective weeks for appreciation depend on rainfall of the previous year.

To view the carpeting of color blessing the desert floor plan to visit during the period of March to early April. Park Rangers will advise you of the best weeks if you will send a stamped and self-addressed postcard, in an envelope, to Wildflowers, P.O.Box 299, Borrego Springs, California 92004. Your self- addressed card will be mailed back to you about two weeks before the expected period of peak blooms. (This is a very special trip and worth its trouble.)

When you plan to visit other areas of Anza-Borrego State Park be sure to purchase a copy of *Weekender's Guide* by Paul R. Johnson. It is an inexpensive and well-written sourcebook to enjoying the best of the entire 600,000 acres.

Anza-Borrego Park **California's Largest State Park**

200 Palm Canyon Drive, Borrego Springs 92004
Information Sources: 767-4684 *Thomas Guide Pg.1078, E/2*

This Visitor Center of the largest state park in the nation (600,000 acres) is the key to enjoying more Secret Sites in San Diego County than can be found in any single area. There is Borrego Palm Canyon with round-trip nature trails, Coyote Canyon with a year-around stream, Font's Point with an astounding overview of the desert, Split Mountain which exhibits a wide variety of geological formations, Mountain Palm Springs with lush palms, the Carrizo Badlands Overlook high above some of natures most twisted landscape and 200 previously unknown elephant trees in the Santa Rosa mountains. Plus opportunities to explore trails used by Spanish explorers of 1774 and 1775, and wagon roads used by emigrants of the 1840s

To view the famous wildflowers at their peak send a stamped/addressed postcard to *Wildflowers, P.O.Box 299, Borrego Springs, CA 92004*. It will be returned to you about two weeks before the flowers reach their full bloom.

Balboa Park **Archery Ranges**

2221 Morley Field Drive, Middletown San Diego 92103
Information Sources: 692-4919 *Thomas Guide Pg.1269, C/6*

There are two major areas in Balboa Park in which archers practice their sport.

A fine Field Archery course is located below the El Prado bridge which spans Freeway 163 through the park. It is entered along a pathway behind the Alcazar Gardens. There are an adequate number of stations allowing individuals and teams to follow each other through the field.

Another archery area is located in Morley Field. There are few signs but it is found to the left of the baseball fields' parking lot as you drive in. Archers are separated from ball players by a stand of high trees. It is a target course with a half-dozen bales at the end of a long range. The use fee is $1.

Balboa Park

Bronze Deed of Gift (1915)

Spreckels Organ Pavilion, Middletown San Diego 92103
Information Sources: 239-0512 *Thomas Guide Pg.1289, D/1*

Adjacent to this dedication is the following bronze deed of gift.

THIS DEED OF GIFT, MADE THIS FIRST DAY OF JANUARY, 1915, WITNESSETH:

In consideration of our appreciation of the good people of San Diego, of our desire to contribute something to their benefit and enjoyment, and of our earnest wish that they may live and prosper in peace and harmony, we, John D. Spreckels and Adolph B. Spreckels, do hereby give and grant, alien and confirm unto Carl I. Ferris, Charles T. Chandler, and John F. Forward, Jr., members of and constituting the Board of Park Commissioners of the City of San Diego, State of California, and to their successors in office forever, all of our right, title and interest in and to that certain organ purchased by us from the Austin Organ Company of Hartford, Connecticut, and to the building wherein it is placed, which we have caused to be constructed, all situated and being in Balboa Park in the said City of San Diego.

TO HAVE AND TO HOLD the same, in trust, nevertheless, for the uses and purposes and with the powers hereinafter mentioned, namely:

FIRST: To keep, insure and maintain the said organ and building for the free use, benefit and enjoyment of the people.

SECOND: If by any change in the laws, the jurisdiction or control of the said Carl I. Ferris, Charles T. Chandler, and John F. Forward, Jr., or their successors as members of said Board of Park Commissioners, over said park shall pass to any other board or body or person, to execute any instrument and do any act necessary or requisite to transfer said organ and building to said other board or body or persons in trust, for like uses and purposes and with like powers.

IN WITNESS WHEREOF, we John D. Spreckels and Adolph B. Spreckels, have hereunto set our hands and seals this the day and year first above written.

Balboa Park

City Christmas Tree

The Mall, Middletown San Diego 92103
Information Sources: 239-0512

Thomas Guide Pg.1289, D/1

This community Christmas tree was dedicated to the people of San Diego on December 25, 1981. Donors included the Community Christmas Center Committee, National Electrical Contractors Association and Masonry and Cement Apprentice Program. The cedar deodara was from the Cunningham Tree Farm.

Balboa Park

El Cid Campeador

The Mall, Middletown San Diego 92103
Information Sources: 239-0512

Thomas Guide Pg.1289, C/1

El Cid Campeador, overlooking the park's Plaza de Panama, is the work of sculptor Anna Hyatt Huntington. It was presented to the City of San Diego on July 5, 1930, by Trustees of the Hispanic Society of America.

Balboa Park

El Prado (1915)

Public Walkway, Balboa Park, Middletown San Diego 92103
Information Sources: 239-0512 *Thomas Guide Pg.1289, B/1*

El Prado, *The Public Way* was the main walkway through the 1915-1916 Panama California Exposition celebrating the opening of the Panama Canal. Two-car electric trains looped around downtown San Diego then ran through Balboa Park to a Park Boulevard station and the main entrance behind the camera. The Cabrillo Bridge in the distance was for motor cars and pedestrians from Middletown.

Balboa Park

Lawn Bowling Courts

El Prado and Balboa Drive, Middletown San Diego 92103
Information Sources: 239-0512 *Thomas Guide Pg.1289, B/1*

These manicured greens are managed by the San Diego Lawn Bowling Club which has offices on the site. There is adequate parking by the courts which are near the Laurel Street end of the Park's Cabrillo bridge entry into El Prado.

Balboa Park

Model Railroads

1649 El Prado, Middletown San Diego 92103
Information Sources: 696-0199

Thomas Guide Pg.1289, C/1

If model trains are a "thing" this museum will be your most important secret site in San Diego. Three local modeler's clubs operate four train layouts six days a week; one in the O scale, one in N scale and two in HO.

The largest permanent layout (O scale) is named the Cabrillo Southwestern and is a San Diego Model Railroad Club project. The same group has the San Diego & Arizona Eastern HO layout which duplicates the existing line from San Diego to Plaster City. Another HO line, by the La Mesa Model Railroad Club is a miniature replica of the Southern Pacific's famous "Tehachapi Loop" where the existing rail line crosses over itself high in the mountains. The fourth permanent layout, Pacific Desert Lines in N scale, is a San Diego N Scale Society project depicting a rail line of the nineteenth century which was surveyed but never built from San Diego to Imperial Valley.

Balboa Park

Nude Nymphs

Casa del Balboa on El Prado, Middletown San Diego 92103
Information Sources: 239-0512 *Thomas Guide Pg.1289, C/1*

High above passers-by along El Prado is a collection of over 20 nude nymphs bracing the roof of the Casa de Balboa. Though somewhat overweight by current standards the nymphs add a delightful feminine touch to the ornate Spanish architecture with its surprising symbolism in portions of the supporting treatment.

Balboa Park

Omnimax Theatre

Plaza de Balboa, Middletown San Diego 92103
Information Sources: 238-1168 *Thomas Guide Pg.1289, C/1*

This was the first Omnimax theatre where motion pictures are shown ten times larger than usually viewed in commercial theatres. The Omnimax domed screen encompasses patrons to the point where the senses accept an illusion of actual participation in the scenes. Screened action includes a trip inside the human body, along the ocean floor, living inside a space shuttle, a sailing trip across the desert and an impressive death-defying journey down steep ski slopes.

Balboa Park

Ordem E Progresso

House of Hospitality on El Prado, Middletown San Diego 92103
Information Sources: 239-0512 *Thomas Guide Pg.1289, C/1*

The Park's House of Hospitality bears a unique statement on the east corner high above El Prado in the legend *Ordem E Progresso*. It could be loosely translated two ways: Once as "Order with Progress" and the other as "Method of Progress." That the motto relates to law enforcement may be symbolized by the generic Sheriff's badge used as decorative treatment just below the legend.

Balboa Park

Spreckels Organ Concerts

The Mall, Middletown San Diego 92103
Information Sources: 239-0512 *Thomas Guide Pg.1289, C/1*

For years free organ concerts have been presented here on each Sunday. This is the organ and pavilion described in the Bronze Deed of Gift (See index).

Balboa Park

Velodrome

2221 Morley Field Drive, Middletown San Diego 92103
Information Sources: 692-4919 *Thomas Guide Pg.1269, C/6*

The San Diego Velodrome (from *velocipede* as in bicycle) Committee of the National Bicycle Association manages this Morley Field Bicycle Track.

There are separate lanes on the track and different starting positions behind the pole line for "sprinters" and for "stayers." All competitors are required to wear helmets, and shoes without cleats. The direction of riding is counterclockwise with weaving or careless passing cause for disciplinary action.

The track is reached by parking in the large lot nearest the baseball fields. Follow the paved walkway along the left side of the ball diamonds to the far end where the velodrome is somewhat hidden in a natural depression of park land.

Balboa Park

Water Tank Gallery

2004 Park Boulevard, Middletown San Diego 92103
Information Sources: 235-6135 *Thomas Guide Pg.1289, C/1*

What was originally a water storage tank for the Balboa Park area was converted into a gallery of art for the Centro Cultural de La Raza. A number of entrances were cut into the outside wall of the circular building at the same time plumbing and electrical services were installed.

As used by the Centro Cultural, the interior displays and preserves the art and culture of Chicanos, Mexicans and Indigenous people of the Americas. Programs include workshops, exhibitions, performing and literary arts presentations and community educational classes.

Balboa Park

Workers' Fountain (1936)

Spreckels Organ Pavilion, Middletown San Diego 92103
Information Sources: 239-0512 *Thomas Guide Pg.1289, C/1*

One of the most unusual memorials in Balboa Park is the "Workers' Fountain" which displays a bronze plaque bearing the inscription *Herein are the signatures of the workers whose untiring and loyal efforts made possible the California Pacific International Exposition 1936*. Water in the fountain basin is frequently used by backpackers and others as the source of a morning wash-up.

Barrio Logan

Chicano Park

1982 National Avenue, San Diego 92113
Information Sources: 236-6661

Thomas Guide Pg.1289, C/5

Some of San Diego's finest folk art is found on supports of the Coronado Bay Bridge where they touch ground along National Avenue by Dewey Street.

According to historical resource reports the site covers four acres under the Bridge intersection with Interstate 5. Recreational facilities are spread from Dewey to Crosby Streets along National Avenue. An interesting kiosk is styled to reflect the designs of Aztec temples. The art on bridge pillars and cross-beams emphasizes historic significance of our Mexican-Americans. The works are well worth a visit.

Original intended use of the land after Interstate 5 was in operation for a number of years was to install a station for the California Highway Patrol. During April of 1970 about 250 residents of the Barrio Logan area camped at the site for twelve days to bring the intended Patrol station project to a halt. In time the City of San Diego acquired the land from the State of California and made good on a promise to create a park for Mexican-Americans. Public art was included in the arrangement and what exists is a stimulating reflection of Chicano ethnic heritage.

Barrio Logan

Flat-Iron Apartments (1911)

National Avenue and 26th Street, San Diego 92101
Information Sources: None *Thomas Guide Pg.1289, D/6*

The Historical Site Board of the City of San Diego describes this building as "Unique to the area and one of the few like it in San Diego. Because the...subdivision was laid out to take advantage of the bay view, this little island was left...at a 45 degree angle...The building was designed and constructed to take advantage of the island. For some 40 years, from about 1920 on, there were...residents living in the upstairs flats. In the early days the (structure was) known as the Flat Iron Apartments and were owned by Mrs. R. May Strong who lived there during the 1920's. Throughout the 1920's there was a downstairs grocery store owned and operated by William F.Sangster. In 1930, during the great experiment with prohibition in the U.S., Sangster converted his grocery store into a wholesale and retail distribution point for malt and hops. By 1934...with the repeal of the 19th Amendment, Sangster had converted the business again, this time to a liquor store. In 1936 the site became a public bar and was called Jack's Island Tavern."

Currently there is a beauty salon in the ground level retail space with apartment dwellers occupying the upper two floors.

Borrego Springs

Christmas Circle

Palm Canyon Drive & County S-3, Borrego Springs 92004
Information Sources: 767-5555 *Thomas Guide Pg.1058 (1078, J/2)*

On Christmas Eve, December 24, 1775, the first white child was born in the Coyote Canyon area to a colonist with the De Anza expedition. On Christmas day the child was baptized. There is a monument in Coyote Canyon honoring the birth site. It is reached over a rough dirt track from the north end of Di Giorgio Road. Inquire at the Park's Visitor Center for an update on current road conditions.

Residents of Borrego Springs named their town's central road junction Christmas Circle in honor of the birth. Currently the Circle is the site of many local activities including street fairs, community celebrations and craft showings.

Borrego Springs

Liar's Monument

S-22 and Henderson Canyon Road, Borrego Springs 92004
Information Sources: 767-5555 *Thomas Guide Pg.1058, H/4*

Legend is that adding ten stones to the pile beyond the signs will bring the donor good luck and success in finding "Peg Leg" Smith's lost mine. That no one has yet found Smith's gold strike leads to questions as to validity of the luck.

Peg Leg, who lived in the area from about 1850 to 1866, was renowned as the teller of tall tales. Each year there is a weekend Liar's Contest around a raging campfire. Prizes are random donations for the most unbelievable stories.

Campo

Gaskill Stone Store (1885)

31130 Highway 94, Campo 91906
Information Sources: 478-5707

Thomas Guide Pg.430, B/10

The Gaskill Brothers Stone Store, built in 1885, was constructed to replace a wooden structure on the same site which had been severely damaged during a raid on the business by bandits.

It is operated as a museum, with a replica of the pioneer store on the ground floor and museum exhibits on the upper floor, by members of the Mountain Empire Historical Society. Most of the exhibits relate to Camp Lockett (1940-1941) which was located nearby as the United States Army's last calvary post. Later Camp Lockett was used to house Italian and German prisoners of war. During 1945 and 1946 it was the site of Mitchell Convalescent Hospital.

Campo

Train Ride In The Hills

Highway 94 & Forest Gate Road, Campo 91906
Information Sources: 697-7762

Thomas Guide Pg.430, B/10

A backcountry train ride from this station is highly regarded as a land voyage through some of San Diego's most historic area. The San Diego Railroad Museum has scheduled runs on weekends. The 16-mile journey in vintage railroad equipment are over rails of the San Diego and Arizona Railway which was completed in 1919 as the direct link between San Diego and the eastern United States. The line is most unique in that a portion of the route is through Mexico which is an international distinction shared with no other railroad.

In addition the railroad museum has a fine collection of historic railroad rolling stock on which restoration work is in progress. Guided tours are provided by Museum volunteers on weekends when tourist trains are in operation.

Cardiff-by-Sea

Graffiti in the Sidewalk

Birmingham Drive at San Elijo , Cardiff-by-the-Sea 92007
Information Sources: 436-0431 *Thomas Guide Pg.1167, D/3*

What could well be termed the County's most creative community development project is demonstrated by seven blocks of sidewalk on Birmingham Drive leading uphill from San Elijo Avenue.

In the mid '80s residents of the area wanted the County to install a sidewalk. The County claimed there were no funds for such an improvement and hinted that the petitioners could install their own concrete. So they did. For $15 a donor could write or draw what they wished on their square of paving. It's worth the trouble to inspect nearly 100 messages that are now in their second decade.

Carlsbad

Celebration

Alga and Alicante Roads, Carlsbad 92008
Information Sources: 634-1334

Thomas Guide Pg.1127, G/6

There's a bit of delightful madness in a vacant field on Alga Road at Alicante as the result of inspiration and hard work by artist Jack B. Quick.

Quick is quoted as saying "It's...something I envision as a celebration to lift people's spirits and give them a happy, joyous feeling when they look at them." Titled *Celebration* the assembly is three oversize figures of aluminum sheet. One is stationary and the other two swing gently in the frequent breeze as though waving to passers-by. (They're genuine fun stuff of which we need more.)

Carlsbad

Crown Lair (1989)

3420 Camino de Los Coches, Carlsbad 92009
Information Sources: 434-2895

Thomas Guide Pg.1147, J/2

A most unusual piece of public art, "Crown Lair", is found in Carlsbad's Stagecoach Park. These softly curving walls adjacent to ruins of what is said to be a former stagecoach station are of stone which gently supports the implied strength of the area's history. It was designed by Lloyd Hamrol in 1989 with a commission from the City of Carlsbad's Art In Public Places Program. Construction was under the direction of Poynter Masonry of Escondido.

Adjacent adobe ruins enclosed in a protective shelter are often referred to as a stagecoach station and source of the park's name. However a newspaper article from 1977 speaks of the adobe as the 1842 Mexican land-grant home of Andres Ybarra who by 1854 valued his surrounding 4431 acres at $3760 including 25 cows, two yoke oxen, seven tame horses 40 mares and one stud.

Carlsbad

Message In A Bottle (1990)

On Carlsbad Boulevard at Sycamore, Carlsbad 92008
Information Sources: 438-7753 *Thomas Guide Pg.1106, E/6*

The City of Carlsbad has a community art program that commissioned Raul Guerrero to complete his "Message in a Bottle" mural (1990) of fired tile on a well-sited bench, It overlooks the Pacific Ocean from an individualized sidewalk veranda on Carlsbad Boulevard between Chestnut and Sycamore Avenues.

Carlsbad

The Village

On Carlsbad Blvd at Cannon Road, Carlsbad 92008
Information Sources: 434-2824 *Thomas Guide Pg.1126, F/2*

In a desire to be known as a small friendly town the City of Carlsbad selected *The Village* as its identity slogan. This board on the north side of Carlsbad Boulevard at Cannon Road has a huge power-generating plant for a backdrop. Most San Diego communities have such slogans but few have it publicly displayed.

Carlsbad

Three-Feet "No Parking"

On Ocean Street at Grand Avenue, Carlsbad 92008
Information Sources: 729-4983

Thomas Guide Pg.1106, D/5

What must be the world's shortest *No Parking* zone is located in the 2800 block of Ocean Street in Carlsbad. Only three feet long, it protects a stairway for residents of a Lutheran retirement facility in what was once known as Carlsbad by the Sea.

Carlsbad

Twin Inns (1887)

2978 Carlsbad Boulevard, Carlsbad 92008
Information Sources: 729-3131

Thomas Guide Pg.1106, D/5

Originally there were a pair of these lovely buildings which were constructed for use as residences by area developers. In 1914 the homes were remodeled into hotel/restaurants known as the "Twin Inns." Later one was torn down leaving the pictured structure to continue serving North County's hungry visitors.

Chula Vista

Gunpowder Point (1916)

1000 Gunpowder Point Way, Chula Vista 91910
Information Sources: 422-2481 *Thomas Guide Pg.1309, H/6*

All that remains of the Hercules Powder Co. plant on the Sweetwater marsh is this pair of sloping concrete barriers on grounds of the Chula Vista Nature Center. This view is from a walkway at the Center. Prior to and during World War I kelp was harvested from nearby San Diego waters and converted into potash inside a building located between the barriers. The barrier slopes are designed to deflect an accidental explosion upward and away from surrounding structures Potash became a critical need during the war as the basis of military explosives. .

From about 1916 to 1920 the San Diego Electric Railway operated "Potash Specials" to bring workmen to the potash plant from both Chula Vista and downtown San Diego. At that time building the spur line to the Hercules plant was reported to have cost a little over $1000. The railway company installed the new tracks (1916) from junction switches located slightly north of interurban rails which remain on F Street near Interstate 5 in Chula Vista.

Chula Vista

Interurban Trolley Rails (1907)

F Street at Interstate 5, Chula Vista 91910
Information Sources: 691-5027 *Thomas Guide Pg.1309, J/7*

On December 1, 1907, the first interurban trolley cars from San Diego rolled into Chula Vista over these rails remaining in the center of F Street east of Interstate 5.

They provided both passenger and freight service and presently connect with track for the San Diego Trolley and separately with track at one time used by the San Diego & Imperial Valley Railroad and the Coronado Railroad.

During San Diego's early years there was excellent interurban electric car service from the Downtown area through National City and inland south to Otay. From there passengers could transfer to a small steam train which provided carriage to the Mexican border and Tijuana. By 1946 all such interurban rail transportation had been discontinued for lack of patronage.

Chula Vista

Konoids

Bayside Park, Chula Vista 91910
Information Sources: 691-5071 *Thomas Guide Pg.1329, H/1*

In 1984 the Port of San Diego unveiled Kenneth Capps' "Konoids" which are located in Bayside Park along Chula Vista's waterfront.

The impressive steelworks lend themselves to imaginary trips of fancy ranging from emerging fungi to the arrival of space travelers. The site provides a most attractive vista over San Diego Bay toward Coronado and the Bay Bridge.

Chula Vista **Nature Center**

1000 Gunpowder Point Way, Chula Vista 91910
Information Sources: 422-2481

Thomas Guide Pg.1309, H/6

This nature center located on the Sweetwater Marsh was dedicated in 1987 with the avowed mission of restoring San Diego wetlands and educating the public as to their importance. Inside the administration building are numerous exhibits which make up the interactive living museum. It is the only such Western facility accredited to the American Society of Museums. There are educational sessions for children, weekly events, guided tours of wetlands and a speakers program.

Chula Vista

Olympic Training Center

Wueste Road, Lower Otay Reservoir, Chula Vista 91910
Information Sources: 291-8802 *Thomas Guide Pg.1293 (1312, A/6)*

This is the first purpose-designed American Olympic Training Center and the warm-weather counterpart to training centers in Colorado Springs, Colorado, and Lake Placid, New York. Installations include a 400-meter track, 50-meter pool, field hockey pitch, six-bay boathouse with a 2000-meter rowing course, nine-tenth mile cycling course, 50-lane archery range, four soccer fields and four tennis courts. Plus housing, kitchens, medical clinic and strength training facility.

Chula Vista

Tallest Free-Standing Flagpole(1981)

2585 Main Street, Chula Vista 91910
Information Sources: 423-0377 *Thomas Guide Pg.1330, B/5*

At 191 feet it's the tallest free-standing flagpole in the nation. A crane, taller than that on the left, hoisted the 20,000 pound steel pole into position in July of 1981.

Coastal Seashores
Various Locations, San Diego County
Information Sources: 521-8036

Private Beaches

Thomas Guide Pg.Various

There are several sections of San Diego beaches which were privatized prior to the State of California restricting the removal of ocean shores from public use.

Two such major private areas are Saint Malo Beach between Oceanside and Carlsbad, and sands in front of the La Jolla Beach and Tennis Club which joins the south end of La Jolla Shores Beach. Posted beaches extend seaward to the tide line and unless otherwise noted walkers may pass around the property by walking in tidal waters. Swimmers are not involved in such restrictions but boating may be prohibited as over Underwater Parks in the La Jolla/Scripps area.

Coronado

20,000 Square-Foot Beach House(1902)

1015 Ocean Boulevard, Coronado 92118
Information Sources: 437-8788

Thomas Guide Pg.1288, H/7

There are 27 bedrooms in this huge beach house built in 1902 for Bartlett Richards, a well-to-do Nebraska sandhills cattleman on Lot 1 of the original Coronado-Oceanside Estates subdivision. There were additions and changes made in 1914 which increased the total area to 20,000 square feet. The property is only 160 feet deep behind 250 feet of frontage. The historic name is the Richards/Dupee Mansion after the first and second owners. It is privately owned and was occupied by President Clinton and family during a visit to San Diego in 1993.

Biological Study Area

Coronado

Silver Strand Boulevard, Coronado 92118
Information Sources: 694-3049

Thomas Guide Pg.1329, F/4

The South Bay Marine Biology Study Area on Silver Strand is bordered by a splendid bicycle trail on one side and San Diego Bay on the other.

Though encompassing less than 30 acres, the wetlands host a wide variety of water fowl. Dikes which project into the harbor are excellent sites from which to bird-watch during low tide when exposed food sources attract the hungry.

Duchess of Windsor Cottage

Coronado

1500 Orange Avenue, Coronado 92118
Information Sources:

Thomas Guide Pg.1308, H/1

The plaque states: *This bungalow was built in 1905. The Duchess of Windsor resided here in 1920 when she was Mrs. Earl W. Spencer. It was relocated by the Hotel Del Coronado with the cooperation of the City of Coronado and the Coronado Historical Society.* In 1993 it was moved closer to the seashore by the Hotel del Coronado and completely restored for public inspection.

Coronado

First US Army Airfield (1911)

Sunset Park on Ocean Boulevard, Coronado 92118
Information Sources: 694-3049 *Thomas Guide Pg.1288, G/7*

At the west end of Ocean Boulevard is Coronado's Sunset Park where a historical monument describes the nation's first military airfield: Rockwell Field.

The field was opened in 1911 by aircraft builder Glenn Curtis as a flying school for Army cadets assigned to pilot the airplanes he was selling to the War Department. The training field was completely an Army facility until 1917 when the Navy established the North Island Naval Air Station. At that time North Island was attached to Coronado by only a narrow spit of sand, the "Spanish Bight." In 1940 the channel between the two was filled to merge North Island with Coronado. North Island NAS supports Naval aviation training on the West Coast.

Coronado

Iron-Cage Elevators (1888)

1500 Orange Avenue, Coronado 92118
Information Sources: 435-6611 *Thomas Guide Pg.1308, H/1*

There are two operator-driven 1888 Otis Elevators in the Hotel del Coronado. This one in the lobby is a most elegant example of "iron-cage" designs of its period.

Coronado

Largest Wooden Building (1888)

1500 Orange Avenue, Coronado 92118
Information Sources: 435-6611

Thomas Guide Pg.1308, H/1

The Hotel del Coronado is said to be one of the largest wooden structures in the nation and is certainly the most famous on the Pacific Coast. When completed there were 750 rooms on a seven and one half acre site. It was built to support the real estate development of Coronado. From about 1903 the "Del" was the site of impressive social events and attractions which included a gambling casino, golf course, polo fields, ostrich farm, Japanese tea garden, a natural history museum and automobile tours. At first the hotel was served by a steam railway from San Diego which was later modernized to become an electric interurban line.

Coronado

Wizard of Oz House (1895)

1101 Star Park Circle, Coronado 92118
Information Sources: 437-8788

Thomas Guide Pg.1288, H/7

This lovely little home styled in the Colonial Revival tradition is well named. Construction was initiated in 1895 by Anna and Alex Lemche with L. Frank Baum recorded as occupying the home in the early 1900s. It was here that he wrote four of his books while enjoying the mild climate of Coronado winters. It has been reported that Baum also wrote a number of plays during the same period. Known as the "Wizard of Oz" house it is privately owned and well cared for.

Corridor

Golden Rule City (1912-23)

4089 Fairmont Avenue, East San Diego 92115
Information Sources: 533-3905

Thomas Guide Pg.1269, H/5

The only memento of the "Golden Rule City" is this East San Diego City Library branch. A plaque to the right of the door explains: *East San Diego The Golden Rule City. 1912-1923. A 5,654.5 acre plateau 400 feet above sea level, lying astride University Avenue. First homes built during the 1880 boom. First P.O. Teralta (High Land). Incorporated as a city of the 6th class Nov. 7, 1912. Largest city of its age in the U.S.A. Pop. 4000. Thirteen City officials. H.M.Hollman of N.C. first mayor. Two schools, three churches, one newspaper, one bank, police station, fire station, 1200 water meters, sewer system, street cars, no paupers, no hobos, no jail, no idle rich. Annexed to City of San Diego Dec. 12, 1923.*

Cuyamaca Park

Miner's Cabin (1891)

Highway 79, Cuyamaca 92036
Information Sources: 765-0755

Thomas Guide Pg.1176, E/7

This over-restored miner's cabin is only a few yards from the site of the Stonewall Mine from which nearly $2 million in gold was removed. In the cabin is a fine display of photographs of mining and life in Cuyamaca City, a community of 500 persons. The population fell to 16 by 1906 and today no traces remain.

Cuyamaca Park
Highway 79, Cuyamaca State Park 92036
Information Sources: 765-0755

Stonewall Mine (1870)

Thomas Guide Pg.1176, E/7

The strike was announced in 1870 as the Stonewall Jackson Mine. Mining operations began in 1886 and continued until about $2 million in gold had been recovered and the vein exhausted by 1892. By the time the Stonewall was abandoned in 1893 the main shaft was 630 feet deep next to to this site of boilers powering the hoist. The adjacent town of Cuyamaca City had a population of 500 which depended on the mine for a livelihood. There are no visible remains of the City, or its hotel and homes which quickly faded away after the mine closed.

Del Mar

Little Orphan Alley

Between 7th & 8th on Stratford Court, Del Mar 92014
Information Sources: 755-9337 *Thomas Guide Pg.1187, F/6*

Del Mar has some of the most imaginatively named streets in San Diego County. *Little Orphan Alley* and *Shippey Lane* (after a newspaper columnist) are between 7th and 9th Streets. And you'll find *Lois Lane* between 12th and 13th Streets.

Descanso

Public Library, Smallest

24617 Viejas Grade Road, Descanso 91916
Information Sources: 445-5279 *Thomas Guide Pg.1236, A/3*

San Diego County's smallest public library is about two people wide and only twice as long on a tiny sliver of land allowing a person-wide fenced walkway.

Downtown SD

Ben Hur Doors (1912)

Off Broadway on 1st and 2nd Avenues, San Diego 92101
Information Sources: 235-0494 *Thomas Guide Pg.1289, A/3*

The large door on the right is paired with another door of equal size on First Avenue. Both open into the 60 by 80-foot backstage area of the Spreckels Theatre. Kooperman's *San Diego Trivia 2* reports that "During big parade scenes such as the one in *Ben Hur*, the actors and horses would rush out (the) Second Avenue (door), run around the back of the theatre on E Street and enter again on First (Avenue)." Today the big doors are seldom opened as the Spreckels has become a motion picture house and dramatic parade scenes are a thing of the past.

Downtown SD

Cab Drivers' Fountain

Driveway to Horton Plaza, San Diego 92101
Information Sources: 239-2200 *Thomas Guide Pg.1289, A/3*

At the far end of the block, by the Doubletree Hotel, the Cab Drivers' Fountain bears a plaque reading *"Proceeds from this fountain have been donated in the name of San Diego's Cab Driver Industry to the San Diego Chapter of Mothers Against Drunk Driving"*. The fountain, with its ten-storey blue obelisk in the center, is the work of Luis Jimenez. A ring of fish and birds spouting water toward the tiled obelisk while spraying into a basin full of donated coins has drawn mixed reviews from local art critics. The other obelisk in downtown San Diego is within a stone's throw behind the camera at the entry to the Horton Plaza complex. It's a 1985 work by the late Joan Brown which has been described as "...a cheery sight, adorned by colorful, whimsical fish, leopard and birds."

Downtown SD

Contractor's Stamp (1892)

G Street Between State & Union, San Diego 92101
Information Sources: None
Thomas Guide Pg.1289, A/3

Downtown's first concrete side walks were laid in the Stingaree in 1884 according to Kooperman's *Trivia 2* which describes this contractor's stamp of 1892 as the earliest known. It's midway in the block on the south side of G Street and reads *Joseph Kelley, Contractor in Cement, Office 964 Fifth Street.*

Downtown SD

Drawbridge to the Lobby

827 C Street, San Diego 92101
Information Sources: 234-5186
Thomas Guide Pg.1289, B/3

With a throwback to the days of Knights in armor, San Diego's Hotel Churchill features exterior and interior design treatments of the period. The entrance to the lobby is over a wooden "drawbridge" bordered with steel torches topped by jeweled crowns. Overhead is a simulated portcullis to drop during times of attack. The lobby has "stone" walls to make Lancelot and Maid Marion feel at home.

Downtown SD

Excalibur

Front and E Streets, San Diego 92101
Information Sources: 557-6640

Thomas Guide Pg.1289, A/3

The Federal Building in Downtown San Diego does its best to enhance Beverly Pepper's sculpture, known as *Excalibur*, for its potential to evoke images of King Arthur's knights and their skyward swords.

Downtown SD

Fire Hydrants, Brass

4th Avenue and B Street, San Diego 92101
Information Sources: Inquire

Thomas Guide Pg.1289, A/3

Being near a fire hydrant which enhances your building is an ego stroke for more than one San Diego business or resident's canine companion.

Several brass hydrants are by the curb on B Street between Fourth and Fifth Avenues with two more (pictured above) at Sixth Avenue and B Street next to the Copley Symphony Hall. There is a "chrome-plated" hydrant in front of the Museum of Contemporary Art at Kettner and Broadway. For being easy to find in Downtown San Diego this collection may serve the visiting fire buff well.

Downtown SD

Gaslamp Quarter

4th,5th,6th Avenue, So. of Broadway, San Diego 92101
Information Sources: 233-5227 *Thomas Guide Pg.1289, B/3-4*

There's no secret to San Diego's Gaslamp Quarter but within its boundaries are dozens of the County's most unique features. It is about two blocks wide and ten blocks long which encourages easy walking. Find the Quarter's Information Office by the Horton-Grand Hotel for information, books and maps. They offer a walking tour which includes tales of ghosts, former brothels, a "Lawyers' Bridge," wonderful Victorian buildings, Chinese Tong houses, hotels of reputation, places to eat, art galleries and a huge second-hand store which is rewarding to explore. In 1980 the Quarter was listed as a National Historic District. Today it is one of San Diego's most popular tourist sites.

It all began back in 1867 when Alonzo Horton began developing New Town San Diego in the area between Broadway and Harborside. His move was successful until about 20 years later when major businesses began building along Broadway and north. This left many wonderful Victorian buildings and hotels available for less than reputable bars, honky-tonks and brothels. Soon Horton's New Town was known as "The Stingaree" because all who ventured there would get stung as they would from swimming in San Diego Bay at that time. A Chinatown also developed in the Market Street area between 3rd and 5th Avenues. It provided gambling and other services for the many Chinese laboring to construct Southern California railroads.

Downtown SD
149 Horton Plaza, San Diego 92101
Information Sources: 239-9311

Jessops' Street Clock (1906)

Thomas Guide Pg.1289, A/3

He's hard to find but by stooping low to view the mechanics of Jessops' wonderful street clock in Horton Plaza one can see a tiny brown bear happily riding back and forth in the mechanism. In the picture below, his dark brown nose protrudes on the right from the lower of two rings. On the left, in the upper of two same-size circles, you find a tiny bell tolling ticks inside the mechanism.

This 21-foot tall clock is topped with a bronze bird, has four faces and 20 dials indicating such information as seconds, minutes, days of the week and time in distant nations. It required 15 months to design and hand-build this wonder in the Jessops' jewelry store. The works are jeweled with stones native to San Diego including tourmaline, topaz, jade and agate; all of which were mined by the Jessop family and cut in their shop. It is said to be the "most completely jeweled and the finest street clock in America...exhibited at the State Fair in Sacramento in 1907...awarded a Gold Medal."

Downtown SD

Lee Highway (1923)

Broadway between Third & Fourth, San Diego 92101
Information Sources: 236-6462

Thomas Guide Pg.1289, A/3

This multi-purpose monument near the fountain of now severely abbreviated Horton Square tells of former President Calvin Coolidge dedicating the *Pacific Milestone* on November 17, 1923. He is reported to have done so by pressing a button in Washington which rang a bell at this site in San Diego.

This milestone was the western end of what was to be *A Southern Transcontinental Highway* between San Diego and Washington D.C. To be known as the *Lee Highway* it left town over a route now used by Interstate 8, then passed through Arkansas and on into Washington. Newspaper reports indicate the project was not really successful as Route 66, from Santa Monica to Chicago, was more popular and the most frequently used cross-country highway.

A plaque states "*The citizens of San Diego in dedicating this Pacific Milestone, November 17, 1923, hereby gratefully acknowledge the untiring efforts of Col. Ed Fletcher in the construction of a southern transcontinental highway.*"

The *Old Spanish Trail,* which connected St. Augustine, Florida, with San Diego is also anchored by an inscription on another side of this milestone.

Downtown SD
Broadway at First, San Diego 92101
Information Sources: 238-6307

Light, Rock and Water (1986)

Thomas Guide Pg.1289, A/3

A most unusual piece of public art, "Light, Rock and Water," fronts a major downtown office building facing toward Broadway at First Avenue.

Completed in 1986 to a design by Charles Ross, the prismatic wall is based by black polished stone in an odd-shaped pond. With water and evening lights it is a charming display of art harmonious with its surroundings.

Downtown SD
600 B Street, San Diego 92101
Information Sources: 234-5600

Private Park for 600 B Street

Thomas Guide Pg.1289, B/3

There's a lovely little park at the corner of 6th Avenue and A Street which is behind the 600 B Street Building. Unfortunately the park is private and meant for use by occupants of the adjoining office space. Nevertheless the landscaping creates a delightful visual oasis amid the concrete towers of downtown San Diego.

Downtown SD

Public Toilet, City's Only

3rd Avenue Between C and D Streets, San Diego 92101
Information Sources: 236-6462 *Thomas Guide Pg.1289, A/2*

If there ever was a secret site, this is it.

The entire City of San Diego has only this one public toilet which is on 3rd Avenue around the corner from the Mayor's office. The facility (toilet) is open and staffed from six in the morning to eleven at night every day of the year.

Earthquake Valley

Scissors Crossing

Highway 78 & County S-2, Anza-Borrego Desert 92036
Information Sources: 767-4684 *Thomas Guide Pg.410, A/11*

The junction of State Highway 78 and County S-2 has this unusual name because of the manner in which the two roads are offset, somewhat like a pair of scissors. It can be easily noted on road maps showing the Rancho Valle de San Felipe by San Felipe Creek. There is a California historical monument here for the Vallecito-Butterfield Stage Station which is 19 miles south on S-2. Otherwise, Scissors Crossing is most unremarkable except for the surrounding land area being mapped as "Earthquake Valley" because it straddles the San Felipe Fault line.

Encinitas

Boat Houses (1929)

726-732 3rd Street, Encinitas 92024
Information Sources: 753-6041

Thomas Guide Pg.1147, B/7

The fabulous Boat Houses of Encinitas wouldn't float if the ocean rose to reach their residential harbor site on Third Street.

From the outside a number of faux pilings are connected by heavy marine rope to define the docking area. Each of the boats is about 15 feet high and is mounted on steel tubes anchored to concrete foundations under the soil. The slight tilt to starboard is intentional to give an air of movement to the 20 feet long crafts which have plaster hull exteriors and two decks. There is a mariner's wheel and oak chart desk in each pilothouse. Each boat has 19 portholes to provide outside views for the below-deck living and dining rooms, the galley and heads.

The Historical Resources Inventory of California's Department of Parks and Recreation describes their importance. "The Boathouses are significant both for their highly unusual design and as the work of the noteworthy local building contractor and retired marine engineer Miles M. Kellogg...builder of a large number of the extant buildings in Downtown Encinitas dating from the mid-to-late 1920's period. These two structures are also of note because they were constructed by Kellogg from some of the wood salvaged from two historic Encinitas buildings demolished in 1928: The Moonlight Beach dance pavilion and the third floor of the first Encinitas Hotel. Despite their authenticity in most details, the Boathouses were not designed as sea-going vessels that were subsequently moved ashore, but as land dwellings never-intended for the water. These structures are landmarks in the truest sense, having been a tourist attraction since the time of their construction...and (the) subject of numerous newspaper articles."

Encinitas
959 Cornish Drive, Encinitas 92024
Information Sources: 755-0500

Egyptian House (1924)

Thomas Guide Pg.1167, C/1

Following the discovery of King Tut's tomb in 1923 a number of homes were built in San Diego County reflecting elements of Egyptian styling.

This home was originally one-storey which was enlarged around 1938 to make room for a pipe organ on the second floor. As built, the structure was white with decorative elements enhanced by brilliant colors. The entranceway is bordered by two papyrus columns. A cobra goddess with vulture wings is above each column, There is a cobra and globe over the entry. There are said to be other elements of the original Egyptian design facing the garden including two pilasters decorated with fruit, vegetables, animal forms and Egyptian hieroglyphics in bas-relief. Such features are historically significant as a fine example of what is termed a "flight of fantasy" by the architect/builder, a Mr. Steele.

Additions include a rather strange bridged fountain in the front yard and two pots on the roof parapets. It is also worth noting a sign-board above the doorway which suggests that "Ocean View" is a second name for the house.

Encinitas

Quail Botanical Gardens

230 Quail Gardens Drive, Encinitas 92024
Information Sources: 436-3036

Thomas Guide Pg.1147, D/5

The gate is open every day of the year from 8 a.m. to 5 p.m. for only a modest fee to enjoy this outstanding feature garden of San Diego County. The unusual landscaping displays over 3000 species of plants ranging from those found in rain forests to desert shrubs. They are arranged into physical and genetic zones for research and enjoyment. A number of permanent demonstration gardens are used for instruction and display of unique plants and arrangements.

The Gardens are recognized throughout the world as one of the most diverse and botanically important plant collections. There are more bamboo varieties here than anywhere else in the nation as well as the largest hibiscus collection in the Western states. Specialty areas include an Herb Garden, Desert Garden, Old-Fashion Garden, Subtropical Fruit Garden, Native Landscape Garden a waterfall and the well-known Palm Canyon.

Encinitas

Swami's Surfing Beach

On 1st Street, south of K Street, Encinitas 92024
Information Sources: 633-2748 *Thomas Guide Pg.1167, C/1*

Swami's, the most famous surfing site in San Diego, has recently been renamed Sea Cliff Park and the pictured sign is no more.

However the new name did nothing to change conformation of the ocean's bottom and enthusiastic surfing continues unabated. If there's one spot to visit, this is it. Long steps lead down from the bluff to the coastline which is a protected environment. At the bottom of the steps go left at low tide for excellent tidepooling over a somewhat rugged rock beach. By the point to the right you will see surfers of every description waiting for the perfect wave to carry them majestically shoreward. There are restrooms and minor picnic facilities here.

Escondido

Lady on the Bench (1990)

114 Grand Avenue, Escondido 92025
Information Sources: 745-2125 *Thomas Guide Pg.1129, J/3*

One of the most delightful public art works in San Diego is "Lady on the Bench", a pair of bronze figures seated on a curbside bench in central Escondido.

Mother and child are resting while mother inspects her purse for the surprise promised her son, a surprise you too can see by looking inside. The $19,000 work by T.J.Dixon was installed on Grand Avenue in 1990. Elementary school students provided its official name of "Reflections on Downtown."

Escondido

Mennisota [sic] Ave.

Seventh and Broadway Streets, Escondido 92025
Information Sources: 743-8207

Thomas Guide Pg.1129, J/3

In the early days of expansion and street construction, Escondido was blessed with a number of unusual street-name misspellings. Another stamp at the same corner has a period after both *Minnesota* and *Ave.*

The stamp shown above is matched by another on the Broadway curbs at Seventh Street in which *Lime TS* is set into the concrete instead of the more correct *Lime St*. It's worth wondering if a laborer was having a bit of fun or just could not spell. Along nearby Maple Street many of the old street name stamps were carefully retained when new paving was installed, a historical preservation effort much to the credit of Escondido's city management.

Escondido

Morteros in the Park

742 Clarence Lane, Escondido 92029
Information Sources: 694-3049

Thomas Guide Pg.1149, J/1

Indian grinding holes are everywhere in San Diego County with those in Felicita County Park being among the most accessible. These morteros are located at the south end of the lower parking lot which is in front of Park Headquarters. It was here in years past where Indian women met to exchange gossip and grind their collected wild acorns, seeds and grains into meal.

Escondido

Wild Animal Park

15500 San Pasqual Valley Road, Escondido 92027
Information Sources: 234-6541

Thomas Guide Pg.1130, J/6

The renowned Wild Animal Park is a 2100-acre complex which, as management says, "Puts visitors in a cage and allows the animals to roam free."

There is an hour-long monorail ride which passes above and through wild animal habitats, a Nairobi Village with animal shows and a garden, a hiking trail through a portion of the park, desert and Bonsai gardens, plus adequate food services and photo opportunities for the most eager. Though somewhat distant from the central city there are motor coach tours and public transportation.

Fallbrook

Masonic Cemetery (1917)

1177 Santa Margarita Drive, Fallbrook 92028
Information Sources: 723-0492

Thomas Guide Pg.1027, G/1

This Masonic Cemetery, completed in 1917, is one of five such California Masonic cemeteries and the only one now in operation. It serves all faiths. A small area with upright stones is the oldest as all current burials use flat headstones.

As a historical archive the cemetery is considered of great value. Headstones record the passing of pioneer families with the size and number of such family stones indicating their importance in the community. An influenza epidemic caused the death of many Fallbrook residents in 1917 and two of the earliest dated stones record final location of the deceased citizens.

Fallbrook

Odd Fellows Cemetary (1881)

Alturas Road and Clemens Lane, Fallbrook 92028
Information Sources: 728-2585 *Thomas Guide Pg.1027, F/4*

William Pittenger, one of the nation's first Medal of Honor recipients (1883), is buried in Plot 15 of Section A in this 236-plot rural cemetery on four acres.

Pittenger was one of a group of Union soldiers who scouted behind the Confederate lines in search of a train they could steal and by so doing damage the South's supply lines. The men were captured. After the Civil War Pittenger wrote a book about the venture. (In 1889 the entire cemetery was sold for $93.)

Fallbrook

Ostrich Creek Bridge (1925)

Overland Trail at Mission Road, Fallbrook 92028
Information Sources: 723-4125 *Thomas Guide Pg.1047, H/1*

The now closed narrow bridge on the west side of Mission Road was named after a Mount Fairview ostrich farm which has long since been gone. The Ostrich Creek Bridge was an important link in Highway 395 that was at one time the primary in-land link between San Diego and Riverside County to the north.

Gaslamp Quarter

Canary Cottage (1903)

530 4th Avenue, Downtown San Diego 92101
Information Sources: 235-9337

Thomas Guide Pg.1289, A/3

This narrow gated walkway at 530 4th Avenue is said to have been the entrance to Madam Ida Bailey's Canary Cottage, a famous parlor house of 1903. When Ida opened the pale yellow house in 1903 it was behind a white picket fence. Legend has it that when commercial structures were built along 4th Miss Bailey had sufficient clout to have the walkway retained to allow entrance to her premises which were on the rear of the lot. Police raids caused her to move elsewhere in 1905. By featuring only the most refined ladies the Canary Cottage hosted many business and political leaders of San Diego. The ladies are reported to have been limited to light make-up, dressed attractively and not been allowed to use vulgar language or allow their guests to do the same. Nor was smoking permitted.

Gaslamp Quarter

Chinese Tong House (1911)

428 3rd Avenue, Downtown San Diego 92101
Information Sources: 235-9337

Thomas Guide Pg.1289, A/3

Though Chinese Tong houses possess an aura of mystery, most are now used by benevolent associations or merchant groups. When home to the Gee Good Tong the building above (1911) is said to have protected planners of the Chinese mainland revolution of 1912. In 1920 the present Benevolent Association emerged from the Tong. The building below (1925) houses a merchant's association.

Gaslamp Quarter

Lawyer's Bridge (1940)

E Street Between 4th & 5th Avenues, Downtown San Diego 92101
Information Sources: 235-9337 *Thomas Guide Pg.1289, A/3*

At one time this was the only such walkway between buildings in the Gaslamp Quarter. The somewhat sloping passway was installed in the 1940s because 901 4th Avenue was the "Lawyers Building" which housed a law library and a title search company. Backing it up was 905 5th Avenue with more attorneys and the County recorder's office to which access was frequently needed.

Gaslamp Quarter

National City & Otay R.R.Depot(1896)

203 5th Avenue, Downtown San Diego 92101
Information Sources: 232-4669 *Thomas Guide Pg.1289, A/4*

What is now a Mexican restaurant was built in 1896 as a passenger and freight depot for the National City and Otay which also provided transportation to the border with Mexico. The interior of the building retains many construction features of its original use as a railroad freight house. During the early period there were eight trains daily between National City and this terminal. In 1908 the Spreckels' interests purchased the line and changed its name to the San Diego and Southeastern Railway. They also had use of the Coronado Railroad tracks which paralleled a part of the SD&S. Soon the old National City line was electrified and interurbans replaced the steam service to Otay. From there steam trains operated to the border. On July 18, 1910 the last regularly scheduled steam passenger train left the San Diego depot for National City and Otay. Later, excursion steam trains traveled over sections of the electrified line or along the Coronado freight rails.

Gaslamp Quarter **Spooks in the Horton Grand (1886)**

311 Island Avenue, Downtown San Diego 92101
Information Sources: 544-1886 *Thomas Guide Pg.1289, A/4*

Roger the spook of the Horton Grand Hotel in San Diego's famous Gaslamp Quarter is best described the "jolly" ghost of Room 309. Though he was not asked to model, note the one curtain pulled aside in the picture above. It is Room 309.

His full name was Roger A. Whittaker, age 37, when he was shot dead while hiding in the armoire of an unnamed San Diego hotel room. Why he was hiding in a bedroom has never been satisfactorily explained although he was said to have been terminated by a gambling "associate" seeking debt repayment.

Be that as it may, Roger is credited with moving pictures, turning lights on and off and dancing on the ceiling while Room 309 was occupied by two San Diego lady psychics. They claimed to have enjoyed his antics although hotel staffers report that more timid guests have checked out during the dark hours after becoming uncomfortable with Roger's presence. It is also said that a few of the hotel's chambermaids refuse to service the room in awe of light switchings and vibrating beds. Another room, this one on the second floor overlooking the central patio, is also said to be haunted but to date no one is quite sure who is doing the haunting though guests speak of white gowned women passing along the porch.

It's worth pointing out that the Horton-Grand is a reconstruction of two older buildings that were located elsewhere. One, the Grand Horton, opened in 1886 to match the boom of early transcontinental train arrivals. The other, the Brooklyn-Kahle Saddlery Hotel at 733 E Street, was so named for a saddle shop which occupied the ground floor for almost 80 years. Both buildings had been targeted for removal by the late 1970s. They were purchased from the City of San Diego for $1, carefully taken apart and reassembled as a single structure at the present location. Roger the spook came with the 10,000-brick hotel-building kit.

Gaslamp Quarter

Stingaree Hotel Site (1887)

538 Fifth Avenue, Downtown San Diego 92101
Information Sources: 235-9337 *Thomas Guide Pg.1289, A/3*

From its time of construction in either 1885 or 1887, depending on which historical research you value most, the two-storey building in the middle was one of the most active brothels in the Stingaree, as the Gaslamp Quarter was known prior to its restoration as a tourist attraction.

The busy upstairs of the Stingaree Hotel opened with only eight rooms rented as living quarters. Though toilets and baths were down the hall the structure soon became a haven for available women. Police raids and attempts to control such activity were common after the "cleanup" of 1912 in which 138 prostitutes were arrested. A report from the Gaslamp Foundation states that "...136 promised to leave to leave the city (and) two agreed to reform their ways. The next morning one changed her mind. The other was found to be insane." Another historian claims the girl who did not change her mind went to work for the City as a telephone operator. During this period the ground floor was variously occupied by a revival center, billiard parlor, employment agency and men's clothing store.

In June of 1980 the Gaslamp Quarter Foundation acclaimed the Stingaree Hotel an "outstanding visual contribution and contemporary application of period architecture." This act honored reconstruction and restoration work which left the building as seen today.

Gaslamp Quarter

Tax Credit Bricks

444 4th Avenue, Downtown San Diego 92101
Information Sources: 234-1234

Thomas Guide Pg.1289, A/4

One of the better stories about the reconstruction of the Gaslamp Quarter concerns bricks used for the Hahn Cosmopolitan Theatre. In 1912 the San Diego Paper Box Company operated a combined factory and warehouse here. During the 1980s the factory building was dismantled and the bricks used to construct this 250-seat theatre on the same site. As a result of reusing original material on the same location a useful Federal tax credit is said to have become available to the builder.

Gaslamp Quarter

The SDG&E Generator Station (1890)

900 Imperial Avenue, Downtown San Diego 92101
Information Sources: 696-2000

Thomas Guide Pg.1289, B/4

This handsome red brick building is thought to be one of the first San Diego public utility structures. SDG&E began in 1881 as the San Diego Gas Company. There were 89 customers in the city of about 3000 residents. When the company began producing electricity in 1887 the name was changed to SDG&E Light Co. San Diego grew rapidly and by 1918 SDG&E connected itself to the Southern California Edison Company at San Juan Capistrano to obtain additional power. The gas producing plant was closed when a natural gas pipeline arrived in 1932.

Gaslamp Quarter

385 5th Avenue, Downtown San Diego 92101
Information Sources: 233-5227

Window of Time

Thomas Guide Pg.1289, A/4

Like almost everything in the Gaslamp Quarter this delightful mural by artist David Robinson represents efforts dating back over a century.

When developers of the Quarter decided on a public art program the owner of this building had the bricks primed so the mural paints would last. Robinson, seeking models for his art, found an 1880s photograph taken in the area for which the photographer "shot" customers from a nearby saloon. Robinson used original print for his seven figures on the left. The man on the right is a current friend given glasses, a mustache and pioneer clothing to match the old timers.

Grantville

4647 Zion Avenue, San Diego 92120
Information Sources: 528-5818

Sinister Garden (1983)

Thomas Guide Pg.1249, J/6

In front of the Kaiser Permanente Hospital you'll find this small but interesting display of plants which destroy one's peace of mind. There's poison ivy, oleander, holly, wisteria, poinsettia and similar unfriendly species. Across the walkway is a garden of medically beneficial plants including foxglove, papaya and pine.

Harbor Island

Spanish Landing (1769)

North Harbor Drive, San Diego 92133
Information Sources: 686-6200

Thomas Guide Pg.1288, E/1

Spanish Landing Park commemorates the 1769 arrival of Spanish explorers in the San Diego area. Crews of the *San Carlos* and *San Antonio* established a camp in early May to await the arrival of overland colonists traveling from Baja California. One party arrived on May 14 and a second group appeared on July 1, 1769. The merging of sailors with the overland parties created a force which began Spain's occupation of what is now California. In fairness, it must be pointed out that some question exists as to exactly where the sailors landed or the overland parties camped. Earlier, Juan Cabrillo was first (1542) to see the bay which he named San Miguel. In 1602 Sebastian Vizcaino arrived and mapped it as San Diego.

Harborside

Dead Men's Point (1782)

Harbor Drive & Pacific Highway, Downtown San Diego 92101
Information Sources: California Landmark

Thomas Guide Pg.1288, J/4

Offically known as *La Punta de los Muertos* this California Historical Landmark is where deceased Spanish sailors and marines were buried in 1782. They were off the royal frigates *La Princesa* and *La Favorita* commanded by Don Augustin de Echeverria who directed the charting and surveying of San Diego Bay.

Harborside

Ferry to Coronado

1300 North Harbor Drive, Downtown San Diego 92101
Information Sources: 234-4111 *Thomas Guide Pg.1288, J/3*

There's a tiny ferry which makes regular trips between Harborside to the ferry landing/shopping center at Coronado. It's a $4 (Round Trip) ride across San Diego Bay. Service begins at 0900 from San Diego and ceases at 2130 from Coronado. Bicycles are $1 (Round Trip) for those who plan to ride the Silver Strand bikeway.

Harborside

Maritime Museum

1306 North Harbor Drive, Downtown San Diego 92101
Information Sources: 234-9153 *Thomas Guide Pg.1288, J/3*

Anchored in the harbor by Downtown San Diego is a highly regarded Maritime Museum displaying an 1863 sailing ship, 1898 ferryboat and 1904 steam yacht.

The *Star of India*, an iron merchantman, was used in the India jute trade and later to transport emigrants to New Zealand from London. The San Diego Maritime Museum which manages this unusual fleet was founded in 1948 "to perpetuate the glories of maritime history." It was formed to take over operation of the *Star of India* which had arrived in San Diego in 1927 from its storage dock in Alameda. It is a fine example of an iron-hulled sailing ship that is fully operational every now and then when it leaves the dock for a cruise around the bay or to venture a short distance into coastal waters of the Pacific Ocean.

The *Berkeley*, a California ferryboat built in 1898, is not operational. She was the first successful propeller-driven ferry on the West Coast. During the 1906 San Francisco earthquake she operated around the clock to rescue refugees from the burning city It is now used as Museum headquarters with the upper deck in original condition for social events. The engine room has been restored so that visitors can inspect the triple-expansion steam engine in motion.

Of the three vessels in the collection, the *Medea* is both the smallest and the most interesting. It is a fully operational steam yacht launched in Scotland in 1904. The relatively tiny steam yacht was originally a social cruiser along the coast of western Scotland. She served in World War I and II before steaming into San Diego harbor in 1973 The *Media* is only 114 feet long with a beam (width) of 17 feet. Though her oil-fired steam engine is rated at 245 horsepower, maximum speed is a modest ten knots an hour.

The Museum is open daily for a minimum fee which encourages unlimited inspection of all three vessels.

Harborside

Martin L. King, Jr. Promenade

Harbor Drive, India to 5th Avenue, Downtown San Diego 92101
Information Sources: 235-2200 *Thomas Guide Pg.1289, A/4*

The early stages of the Martin Luther King, Jr. promenade indicate this will be a highly regarded point of civic pride opposite the San Diego Convention Center.

It is a six-block-long strip of land between Harborside Trolley tracks and buildings of the Gaslamp Quarter. The program to complete the promenade includes specialized plantings, a reflecting pool and serpentine walkways.

Harborside

Rowing Club (1902)

525 East Harbor Drive, Downtown San Diego 92101
Information Sources: 233-7391 *Thomas Guide Pg.1289, A/4*

Adjacent to the small traffic circle as you enter Marina Park is the former San Diego Rowing Club which was at one time the hub of sporting activity and a social center for the city's most influential citizen-members.

Today it is a fine restaurant which maintains historic flavor of the buildings original use. From its windows diners can watch activity in the nearby marina or observe ocean-going shipbuilding in the adjoining dry-dock. The San Diego Convention Center and Gaslamp Quarter are within walking distance.

Harborside

San Francisco Ferry (1898)

1306 North Harbor Drive, Downtown San Diego 92101
Information Sources: 234-9153 *Thomas Guide Pg.1288, J/3*

The California-built ferryboat *Berkeley* of 1898 was the first successful propeller-drive ferry operating on the west coast. For 60 years she traveled between San Francisco and Oakland on a daily basis.

The *Berkeley* is a National Historic Landmark as much for her age and condition as for the Victorian decorative treatment of the passenger areas. Much of the original woodwork has been restored and stained-glass clerestory windows of the upper deck are works of art within themselves. While in ferry service there was a restaurant below the main deck and a "Ladies Deck" on the upper level.

The conversion from coal to oil was completed in 1900 and in 1918 the simple Scotch boilers were replaced with water-tube boilers similar to those on main-line railroad engines. The engine room has been completely restored and the engines are frequently motored to provide an illusion of the original operation. Described as "the best preserved 19th century ferryboat in existence" her decks are often rented for weddings and social events.

Harborside

Steam-Powered Yacht (1904)

1306 North Harbor Drive, Downtown San Diego 92101
Information Sources: 234-9153 *Thomas Guide Pg.1288, J/3*

This charming steam yacht was built within 51 days in Scotland in 1904. She is equipped with a 254 horsepower compound-reciprocating steam engine and an oil-fired boiler conversion (from coal) of 1964. Maximum cruising speed is about 10 knots with 8-1/2 knots the most economical.

The *Medea* was originally used for cruising the islands of western Scotland but on the arrival of World War I she was purchased by the French Navy. As the gunboat *Corneille* she was equipped with a 75mm cannon, depth charges and a balloon hoist to serve as an escort for convoy's of French merchant ships. After the war she was renamed *Medea* and based in Gibraltar as a pleasure cruiser. She was requisitioned by the British Royal Navy during World War II for duty at the mouth of the River Thames. Later she was used as a base ship for commandos attacking the Norwegian coast. In 1946 the *Medea* again became a privately owned charter yacht until 1971 when she was purchased by Paul Whittier, an American, who completed restoration and donated her to the Maritime Museum in 1973.

Tuna Harbor

Harborside
1 Tuna Lane, Downtown San Diego 92101
Information Sources: 233-6405

Thomas Guide Pg.1288, J/3

San Diego's one-time major commercial activity, tuna fishing, has now been relegated to a tiny section of dockage where a few fishing boats are maintained on docks adjacent to offices of the American Tuna Boat Association.

It is worth a visit to inspect maritime eras past, enjoy lunch or dinner at the restaurant and take home fresh fish from one of San Diego's best markets.

In-Ko-Pah Desert Outlook (1922)

Hell's Canyon
In-Ko-Pah Road, Jacumba 91934
Information Sources: 694-3049

Thomas Guide Pg.430, F/9

Wagon-train pioneers on their way to California named the area east of here "Hell's Canyon" and as viewed by motorists on Interstate 8 the miles of hills and huge boulders could well be from Satan's domain. Near Mountain Springs Road it is possible to locate the original wagon road winding its tortuous path along the south rock cliffs.

In-Ko-Pah Desert Outlook was built to commemorate completion of the first motor road between what is now Imperial Valley and San Diego. From its tower viewers overlook spectacular areas of the southern portion of Anza-Borrego State Park. In addition walkers will find that boulders surrounding the tower have been carved and modified to present the appearance of animals. The carvings are scattered and their discovery is well worth the searching.

The story of their making is on a bronze plaque reading *Desert Tower. Bert Vaughn of Jacumba built the stone tower in 1922-23 to commemorate the pioneers and road and railroad builders who opened the area. In the 1930's W.T.Ratcliffe carved the stone animal figures which lurk in the rocks surrounding the tower, creating a fantasy world of surprise and strange beauty. This remarkable sculptural assemblage is one of California's exceptional folk-art environments. California Registered Historical Landmark No. 939.* The tower is not listed in the current State book *California Historical Landmarks.*

The Desert Outlook has been closed but could be open. Local inquiry is recommended. Use the Jacumba/Carrizo Gorge Road exit from Interstate 8. At the bottom of the offramp drive north to In-Ko-Pah road then east to where it ends at the Desert Outlook. There is a service station at the off-ramp for guidance.

Heritage Park

Victorians in the Park (1887-1893)

Heritage Park Row, Old Town San Diego 92110
Information Sources: 525-8281 *Thomas Guide Pg.1268, F/5*

This lovely Victorian Village is only a stone's throw from Old Town San Diego and in it are some of the finest structural restorations in the County. The display is the result of concentrated effort by concerned citizens who formed the Save Our Heritage Organization. Here you will find the Italianate style Bushyhead home of 1887, the Queen Anne style Christian House of 1889, the 1893 Classic Revival Burton House, a "widows walk" on the Sherman Gilbert House of 1887, the Italian Renaissance style McConaughy House built in 1887 and the Senlis Cottage which was completed in 1893 for Eugene Senlis.

On the right as you enter is San Diego's first synagogue, built in 1889 in the Classic Revival style for Congregation Beth Israel formed in 1861. The first service in this building took place on September 25, 1889. It is the oldest synagogue in Southern California and the building was moved here in 1978.

The Bushyhead house was constructed as a boarding house in 1887. The owner-builder, Edward Bushyhead, was an early deputy sheriff and part owner of the *San Diego Union* newspaper. The building was re-sited here in 1976.

"Ornate" well describes Harfield Christian's house built in 1889. He was a major player in San Diego politics in addition to acting as a U.S. Commissioner, president of the San Diego Title Insurance Guarantee & Trust Co and owner of considerable city property. In 1923 the building was sold and subsequently became a rooming house. The move to Heritage Park took place in 1976.

The estimated date of construction for the Burton House is 1893. It was built for Dr. Henry Burton an opthamologist who had retired from the U.S.Army and settled in San Diego. After a number of owners it was relocated in Heritage Park in 1976 along with the Christian House.

A third floor "widows walk" and unusual window treatments on the 1887 Sherman-Gilbert house are said to be the only remaining examples in San Diego. There is extensive carving on outside decorative trim which has been carefully preserved. Construction costs totaled $20,000 which, for 1887, made it a most expensive home for real estate dealer John Sherman. This structure was purchased by the Save Our Heritage Organization and donated to the County of San Diego. Relocation to Heritage Park took place in 1971.

By comparison it cost only $3500 to build the McConaughy house in 1887. John McConaughy was a pioneer who established freight wagon and passenger stage services between San Diego and Julian. Relocation was in 1981.

Smallest of the Heritage collection is the Senlis Cottage of 1893. It is said that mail-order plans were used. As built, there is only one closet, window catches are of cast-iron and there is no fireplace for heating. During early years it is said to have been occupied by an associate of Kate Sessions, San Diego's highly regarded horticulturist. In 1940 the cottage was divided into a duplex for rental income and eventually was moved into Heritage Park in 1978.

Imperial Beach — Most Southwesterly City

825 Imperial Beach Boulevard, Imperial Beach 91932
Information Sources: 423-8300 *Thomas Guide Pg.1349, G/1*

Almost all cities in San Diego County have one or more slogans describing their assumed or actual virtues. "Most Southwesterly City in Continental U.S." describes Imperial Beach accurately. Its City Limits are about two miles from the border with Mexico. The two-miles are partially controlled by the Navy for helicopter landings, by the Federal Government as a nature preserve and by California's Border Field State Park. Though City Limits of San Diego are against the border in the San Ysidro area (East of Imperial Beach), San Diego's Civic Center is far north leaving Imperial Beach's "Most Southwesterly" title intact.

Imperial Beach — Sand Dunes

South end of Seacoast Drive, Imperial Beach 91932
Information Sources: 575-3613 *Thomas Guide Pg.1349, E/2*

There's about two miles of Pacific beach sand dunes between the southern city limits of Imperial Beach and the Mexican border. They are reached by driving south on Seacoast Drive to roadside parking areas.

The dunes are located in the Tijuana River National Estuarine Research Reserve and terminate south of California's Border Field State Park. Because of their unique formation they are a protected area and trespassing is prohibited. However they can be easily viewed while walking the beach. Swimming is not encouraged in this section due to water contamination from a sewage outfall.

Imperial Beach

Wildlife Refuge, National

301 Caspian Way, Imperial Beach 91932
Information Sources: 575-1290

Thomas Guide Pg.1349, F/1

Three agencies are involved in operation of the Tijuana Estuary which is a major wetlands refuge between Imperial Beach and the Mexican border. They are the Fish and Wildlife Service of the Department of the Interior, California Sea Grant College Program of the U.S.Department of Commerce and California's Parks and Recreation Department

It is unique among the world's estuaries for being a highly variable system which during times of heavy rainfall is fed with fresh water streams. During other periods ocean tides maintain a high level of salinity. Salt marsh vegetation predominates although as the wetlands stretch inland there are dominant areas of chaparral and coastal scrub brush.

Bird life is a feature of the Estuary and the use of powerful field glasses or tripod scopes will reward the user with sightings of many unusual species. Much of the area is restricted and entry is limited to marked paths and boundary lines. Equestrian use is permitted on trails and along the beach frontage which dictates that walkers exercise caution and be ready to provide right-of-way.

Jacumba — Massacre at Jacumba (1880)

State Highway 94, Cameron Corners 91906
Information Sources: 478-5707

Thomas Guide Pg.1318, C/5

William McCain's death is described as the cause of a "massacre" resulting from a confrontation between Indians and white settlers. McCain and his friends from Campo believed that Indians had stolen their horses. The Americans armed themselves and tried to reclaim the stock. McCain was shot during a heated discussion with the Jacumba Indians. As a reprisal the settlers are said to have killed five (one report claims 18) Indians. This burial site is on private property.

Jamul — Burma Shave Signs

Campo and Jefferson Roads, Jamul 91935
Information Sources: 669-1977

Thomas Guide Pg.1292, H/2

Long gone but not forgotten the famous *Burma Shave* signs familiar to cross-country travelers of the mid-century now exist on a Jamul roadside.

As an attention-gaining device for Simpson's Garden Town Nursery this row can be seen on the south-east corner of Highway 94 and Jefferson Road.

Julian

Eagle and High Peak Mines (1870)

Old Miners Trail off C Street, Julian 92036
Information Sources: 765-0036 *Thomas Guide Pg.1136, B/6*

More a tourist attraction than remnants of historic mines, the Eagle and High Peak site is now a collection of buildings, old mining equipment and a tunnel.

Both mines were discovered by former Confederate soldier Drue Bailey. He located the High Peak mine on March 11, 1870, and the Eagle mine shortly thereafter. Bailey was responsible for having the booming town surveyed and named "Julian" in honor of Mike Julian said to have been the handsomest man in the gold mining camp.

Mine names ranged from the simplistic to the exotic. The Washington Mine was discovered on Washington's Birthday. Among others there was the Good Hope, Helvetica, California, Stonewall Jackson, The Golden Chariot, Ready Relief, Owens, Cincinnata (sic) Belle, Warlock, Antelope, Blue Bell, Madden, Hubbard, Kentuck (sic), Tom Scott and the Redman mine

During the first years Julian mining was simply digging and moving the ore off site on pack animals or in some instances panning for gold in the many streams off hills around Julian. In 1873 a major investment in the Golden Chariot mine increased its production to nearly two million dollars. Other small diggings were soon purchased by eager investors and Julian production was expanded.

Eventually there were ten stamp mills in continuous operation. The Wells Fargo office processed shipments of bullion to San Francisco and San Diego. Records are incomplete but the best estimates are that from six to eight million dollars worth of gold came out of Julian's mines. By 1900 the boom had slowed and only a few larger mines continued modest production until 1906.

Today the machinery and diggings of the Eagle and Washington Mines are the main remnant of the gold boom. Julian's economy is supported by visitors and a well-deserved reputation for producing excellent apple pie in a wide variety of configurations. It's a pleasant one day round-trip from San Diego through some of the County's most beautiful countryside.

Julian
Townsite of Julian, Julian 92036
Information Sources: 765-0227

Julian Historic District

Thomas Guide Pg.1136, B/7

This unimpressive road sign announces entry into a complete townsite which has been declared a historic district with building and restoration restrictions to maintain significant values of the community. Gold was discovered in the Julian area in 1870 and within a few years the town had over 200 homes, a number of hotels, saloons and its lovely cemetery on the hilltop. By 1906 the mines had closed and today Julian is one of San Diego's most popular one-day driving trips.

Julian
Main and C Streets, Julian 92036
Information Sources: 734-5854

Oldest Original Hotel (1887)

Thomas Guide Pg.1136, B/7

The Julian Hotel was founded in 1897 as the Robinson Hotel by freed black slave Albert Robinson. It is believed to be the oldest continually operating hotel in San Diego County. There have been additions. That to the right in front is an upgrading but on the whole the facility retains its historic charm. Overnight guests are pleasured with a full breakfast in a dining room crammed with antiques and not-so-old ambience. There are reports of ghostly activities in Room 10 although hotel management is reluctant to discuss nocturnal mischief from Albert's visits.

Julian

Witch Creek School (1888)

2133 4th Avenue, Julian 92036
Information Sources: 765-0370

Thomas Guide Pg.1136, B/7

Though identified as "The Witch Creek School" this building was originally the Santa Ysabela School located about ten miles west of Julian in the community of Witch Creek (*Thomas 409, J/11*). It was in use from 1888 to 1954. In 1970 it was moved to this site and restored for use as the Julian County Public Library.

La Jolla

Bird Rock

West end of Bird Rock Avenue, La Jolla 92037
Information Sources: 459-5335

Thomas Guide Pg.1247, F/4

Bird Rock, so named for the great number of our feathered friends who have coated it with their residue, is an unimpressive lump just a few feet off the La Jolla coastline. Nevertheless, Bird Rock Avenue has been legitimatized and coastal access provided by nearby steps leading down to a narrow shoreline.

La Jolla Cable-Stayed Footbridge (1994)

La Jolla Shores Drive & Downwind Wy, La Jolla 92037
Information Sources: 452-4086 *Thomas Guide Pg.1227, H/3*

This beautiful footbridge is another first for California and intended to be both useful and an innovative approach to modifying current-practice highway bridge building which is presently mired in concrete overkill. There are no stubby pillars under cable-stayed bridges of this type which are frequently found in other nations. A vehicle bridge of similar design is planned for future construction in the area.

La Jolla Children's Sea Pool

Coast Boulevard at Jenner Street, La Jolla 92037
Information Sources: 221-8899 *Thomas Guide Pg.1227, E/6*

This special La Jolla beach area is behind a hooked seawall by a lifeguard tower on stilts with toilets below. The Children's Pool provides an opportunity for small fry to play in ocean waters with a maximum of safety. The seawall gives adults a view of ocean water while birds perched on rocky shores watch the world happen.

La Jolla

Red Roost/Rest Cottages (1894)

1179-87 Coast Boulevard, La Jolla 92037
Information Sources: 459-5335 *Thomas Guide Pg.1227, F/6*

Built in 1894, these now sad appearing buildings were at one time the epitome of beach-front holidaying. One story speaks of George Levy as the builder-owner of both. The La Jolla Historical Society reports two separate original owners with one building being named the *Red Rest* and the other the *Red Roost*.

La Jolla

San Carlos Trolley Station(1924)

6063 La Jolla Boulevard, La Jolla 92037
Information Sources: 454-7108 *Thomas Guide Pg.1247, F/3*

The central two-storey portion of this building was modeled after the San Carlos Mission (Carmel, California) for use as one of two passenger stations on the trolley line between San Diego and La Jolla. Curved walls in the front park area include seats for passengers waiting for the cars. Fine detailing and decorations are outstanding. One-storey buildings attached on the sides are later additions. The site and structures are owned and used by the La Jolla Methodist Church.

La Jolla

Seashore Caves

1325 Coast Boulevard, La Jolla 92037
Information Sources: 454-6080

Thomas Guide Pg.1227, F/6

Two cave explorations are possible in the La Jolla coastal frontage. The easiest, although you might not agree after hiking back up endless steps pictured above, is through the Cave Shop on Coast Boulevard. At the bottom of their steps is a large platform from which you can view the ocean through a cave mouth.

Other, and larger, shoreline caves may be visited during periods of low tide. (Telephone 221-8884). Find public access steps at the intersection of Spindrift Drive and Roseland Avenue (*Thomas 1227, G/5*). At the bottom of the steps walk left, exercising diligence over slippery rocks near the tidepools.

La Jolla

Trolleyway Bike Trail

Nautilus Street at Fay Avenue, La Jolla 92037
Information Sources: 459-5335

Thomas Guide Pg.1247, F/1

This mile-long paved strip between Nautilus Street and Via del Norte was the roadbed for rail services into La Jolla via Fay Avenue. At first a tiny steam engine towed passenger cars to and from San Diego. Then a motor car named the "Red Devil" provided service until replaced in later years by electric cars using the same rails. Today it's a portion of the Pacific Coast Bicentennial (Bike) Route.

La Jolla Point — Underwater Parks

La Jolla Point/Torrey Pines, La Jolla 92037
Information Sources: 755-2063(State), 221-8899(City) *Thomas Guide Pg.1227, G/1*

An underwater park established for scuba and snorkel diving extends from the Torrey Pines area (*Thomas 1207, G/2*) south to La Jolla Bay (*Thomas 1227, F/5*), a distance of about five miles along San Diego's most impressive coastline.

Underwater treasure hunts and the October "Underwater Pumpkin Carving" contest are a part of ocean-oriented events taking place in the site. To protect divers and swimmers boats must not be closer than 100-feet, are limited to five miles an hour and in some portions are totally prohibited. All plants, marine life, geological formations and archaeological artifacts are protected by law.

Lemon Grove — Lemon, World's Largest (1928)

Corner of Broadway & Lemon Grove, Lemon Grove 91945
Information Sources: 469-9621 *Thomas Guide Pg.1270, G/6*

What must be the world's largest lemon is a feature of one of the County's smaller cities. During its early years time Lemon Grove was an agricultural community enjoying frequent daily steam-train service to San Diego with connections to the rest of the United States. Currently the railroad line next to the lemon is used by the San Diego Trolley to provide commuter transportation. The slogan, "Best Climate On Earth," is hotly contested by other communities of San Diego County.

Leucadia

Charlie Chaplin House (1925)

1448 Neptune Avenue, Leucadia 92024
Information Sources: None

Thomas Guide Pg.1147, A/3

This neo-classical two-storey home on the edge of the Pacific Ocean was built in 1925 and shortly thereafter purchased by Charlie Chaplin for his mother. It is considered to be an elegant example of classical revival architecture. Privately owned, it is not open for inspection.

Leucadia

Log Cabin Motor Courts (ca. 1930)

1660 Old Highway 101, Leucadia 92024
Information Sources: 753-6711

Thomas Guide Pg.1147, A/3

These somewhat hidden motel cabins are said to have been nominated for inclusion in the National Register of Historic Places.

They are thought to have been constructed in the mid-30s with surface trim log siding as the distinguishing feature which gives each unit the individual aspect of a north-western frontier building.

Leucadia

Temple Grove Spiritualists (ca.1880)

800 Old Highway 101, Encinitas 92024
Information Sources: 633-2740 *Thomas Guide Pg.1147, A/4*

The County's smallest park, known as Leucadia Roadside Park, was originally the site of worship for a group of British spiritualists who had a temple in the area during the late 1880s. Many area streets have classical names (Jupiter, Glaucus, Cadmus, Diana) for which the spiritualists are given credit. During a 1920s boom period the park was to be the Civic Center for a real-estate subdivision project.

Linda Vista

Stork on the Roof

7901 Frost Street, San Diego 92123
Information Sources: 541-3400 *Thomas Guide Pg.1249, B/5*

The 18-foot landmark Stork on the Sharp Hospital is the symbol of its Woman's Center and the bustling maternity facility which is the State's second busiest birth center. The big bird was found on a 1960 Pasadena Rose Bowl Parade float then donated to the hospital by the city of Sierra Madre. The framework was strengthened by the hospital's Chief Engineer and the bird repainted by a lady member of the Auxiliary based on sketches of storks in the San Diego Zoo.

Lindbergh Field

Airplane/Highway Traffic Signal

Harbor Drive at Laurel Street, Harborside San Diego 92103
Information Sources: 557-6556 *Thomas Guide Pg.1288, H/1*

Visitors are often surprised to see this unusual sign by the side of Harbor Drive adjacent to Lindbergh Field at the Laurel Street intersection.

The traffic signals directly ahead, which are usually green, will change to red when aircraft of the Goast Guard must cross from their hanger on the left (south) to the Lindbergh runway on the right (north). It doesn't happen often but when it does the sight of a huge airplane taxiing across Harbor Drive while vehicular traffic heading for the airport impatiently waits is not easily forgotten.

Logan Heights

Villa Montezuma (1887)

1925 K Street, San Diego 92102
Information Sources: 239-2211 *Thomas Guide Pg.1289, C/4*

Of all Victorian homes remaining in San Diego, Villa Montezuma is considered to be the most outstanding. It was constructed in 1887 under the direction of Jesse Shepard at that time an internationally known author, spiritualist and musician. He was responsible for selection of design treatments which today invoke memories of the past. Shepard was sponsored by wealthy San Diegans who enjoyed elegant dinner parties and entertainment in the Villa. He left San Diego after a few years and today the stately home is managed by the San Diego Historical Society. It's a great place to visit and wonder about rumors of secret passages, ghosts and the mysterious happenings in the Villa's checkered history.

Middletown SD
1572 Columbia Street, San Diego 92101
Information Sources: 232-3473

Firehouse Museum (1911)

Thomas Guide Pg.1289, A/2

A non-profit organization, the Pioneer Hook & Ladder Company founded in 1962, has lovingly restored San Diego Fire Department's Station 6 which is now the home of many unusual exhibits. Displayed are artifacts of the history of San Diego fire protection in a setting designed to interest children and adults.

Included in the collection is an 1841 Rumsey hand pumper which had to be filled by citizen volunteers forming a bucket brigade during fire fighting episodes. Also on display is the only remaining example of San Diego's many hand-drawn fire engines. Perhaps the most interesting is a 1903 Metropolitan steam-powered pump which was pulled to fire scenes behind three horses.

Other exhibits include nearly 50 miniature models of fire fighting trucks and steam pumpers, with many antique bells, alarms, speaking trumpets and extinguishers. It is said that the Pioneer Company's collection of fire department shoulder badges is the largest in the area. Supporting the badges is a display of many rare firemen's uniforms and helmets from other nations.

Middletown SD

Landing On The Roof

1925 5th Avenue, San Diego 92103
Information Sources: 234-4488

Thomas Guide Pg.1289, A/2

Every aircraft approaching San Diego's Lindbergh field passes over a simulated crash-landing on the roof of this 5th Avenue commercial building. The tail section is reported to be from a Cessna that was sold as being no longer air-worthy.

Middletown SD

Macaroni Sidewalk Stamp

2308 Kettner Boulevard, San Diego 92103
Information Sources: 232-6203

Thomas Guide Pg.1288, J/1

Though not an earthshaking item of historical significance this unusual record of commercial nostalgia demonstrates the pride that early San Diego business people found in their enterprise. It's in the sidewalk in front of the building.

Middletown SD

People-Built Bridge (1931)

2700-2800 First Avenue, San Diego 92103
Information Sources: 533-4040

Thomas Guide Pg.1269, A/7

When the residents in the First Avenue and Olive Park area wanted a new bridge they paid for it themselves by floating a bond issue paid by taxes on their homes.

Bronze plaques at each end bear San Diego's City Seal with the motto *Semper Vigilans* (Always Vigilant) and the legend: *A.D. MCMXXI (1931). First Avenue Bridge: Length 463.24 Ft. Height 104. Ft. Erected by property owners under "Improvement Act of 1911". R.E.Hazard Contracting Company.*

Middletown SD

Quince Street Bridge (1905)

1st Avenue at Quince Street, San Diego 92103
Information Sources: 236-7181

Thomas Guide Pg.1269, A/7

As one of the City's oldest bridges, this 236-foot-long wooden structure is continually used by pedestrians in the area. It spans a deep canyon of palm and eucalyptus trees amid hiking trails which were previously used by equestrians.

Middletown SD

Spruce Street Bridge (1912)

Spruce Street off Front Street, San Diego 92103
Information Sources: 236-7181 *Thomas Guide Pg.1269, A/7*

When residents of the Brant Street area needed a means to reach trolley cars on Fourth Avenue, the City responded in 1912 with this four-foot-wide 375-foot-long suspension bridge 70 feet above the canyon. Engineering specifications include the requirement to support the equivalent of 2186 persons averaging 150 pounds.

Middletown SD

Three Sisters

3018-30-42 State Street, San Diego 92103
Information Sources: Private Homes

Thomas Guide Pg.1268, H/7

Three identical homes built during 1913 for a reported total of $11,500 overlook San Diego Bay from this one-block length of State Street. Over the years minor modifications have changed the exteriors slightly but the Sisters' sameness is easily validated by comparing the location and size of doors and windows.

Mission Bay

Fiesta Island

Fiesta Island Road at Sea World Dr., San Diego 92109
Information Sources: 221-8900

Thomas Guide Pg.1268, D/2

Fiesta Island in the central area of Mission Bay was man-made from dredgings which changed the former lagoon (Known as False Bay) into the fine recreational area that it is today.

The driveway onto Fiesta Island leads to a one-way counter-clockwise road around the perimeter. There is plentiful parking, comfort facilities and endless opportunities to watch water-skiing, windsurfing, sail boats and other watercraft. The island is also home to the world-renowned OTL (Over The Line) games held annually. More than 1000 three player teams compete in an air of fun that covers the entire island. There are divisions for men, women and youths.

Mission Bay

Skiing in San Diego

Ingraham at Vacation Road, San Diego 92109
Information Sources: 221-8899

Thomas Guide Pg.1268, B/2

Skiing in San Diego is most frequently accomplished on waters of Mission Bay off Ski Beach which has a large car park, restrooms and picnic facilities. Most importantly, random swimming is not allowed and the beach area is restricted to boat launching and water skiing. One end of the beach frontage is limited to "Take Off" and the opposite end is for "Landing" by water skiers.

During the rare regional snowfall, cross-country skiing is said to be possible on fire roads in mountain areas of the Los Coyotes Indian Reservation.

Mission Bay Park

Kite Flying

1100 East Mission Bay Drive, San Diego 92109
Information Sources: 525-8221

Thomas Guide Pg.1268, D/2

Kite flying in the San Diego area is a common sport along East Mission Bay Drive about 200 yards south of the Hilton Hotel. The site is favored with a near-constant off-sea breeze over a grassed area which facilitates launching complicated kites.

The San Diego Kite Club meets here often for competition and display of the member's creations. The best route is to leave Interstate 5 at Sea World Drive and drive west toward the coast. At Fiesta Island Road turn right and follow East Mission Bay Road north about one-half mile to the kite flying area on the left.

Mission Beach Plunge (1925)

Mission Beach
3115 Ocean Front Walk, San Diego 92109
Information Sources: 488-3110
Thomas Guide Pg.1267, H/3

When opened in May of 1925 this was the largest salt-water plunge in the world though there were plunges in Ocean Park and Venice that were nearly as large.

In 1951 it was switched from salt to fresh water. A number of Hollywood swimming pictures featuring Esther Williams and Johnny Weissmuller were filmed in the 60 by 175-foot pool. The interior is in its near-original condition as compared to the exterior which was completely rebuilt in 1988.

Roller Coaster (1925)

Mission Beach
3190 Mission Boulevard, San Diego 92109
Information Sources: 488-1549
Thomas Guide Pg.1267, J/3

The National Register of Historic Places lists San Diego's Belmont Roller Coaster which is located just a few feet from a wide expanse of Mission Beach sand. It is one of very few old-time coasters left in the United States.

There is a tiny museum by the coaster which details much of its history. Its first name was *The Giant Dipper* after a similar coaster in Venice, California. It was completed in 1925 during a period when coasters were also operating in Balboa Park, Ocean Beach and Coronado. The Belmont was restored and reopened in 1990. There are food concessions, a plunge and carousel in the same complex.

Mission Hills

Pioneer Cemetery Public Park (1873)

Washington Place and Randolph Street, San Diego 92103
Information Sources: 236-6323 *Thomas Guide Pg.1268, H/5*

One of San Diego's most unique public works is Pioneer Park underneath which is Calvary Cemetery. Such use is allowed under California law permitting public benefit conversion of cemeteries unused for a number of years.

Municipal records disclose that on October 27, 1873, the City of San Diego paid $5000 for these ten acres of land to be used as a city cemetery. Though many of San Diego's best known pioneers were buried here, by 1930 the site was no longer maintained. In 1965 the cemetery was placed under jurisdiction of the Parks and Recreation department. Landscaping, rest rooms, picnic facilities and children's recreation equipment have been installed.

A panel of six large marble plates bear names of all known to have been interred. Behind the memorial are about 150 selected headstones as a historically significant monument to the site's original use.

Mission Trails Pk

Mission Dam (1813)

Father Junipero Serra Trail, San Diego 92124
Information Sources: 694-3043

Thomas Guide Pg.1230, F/6

A plaque near the damn reports *Built in 1813...a part of the first permanent irrigation system project by Padres and Indians of California.*

Today it is a lovely site to visit or, as some do, drop a line into the running San Diego River stream and hope no fish will bite to disturb your peace of mind. The surrounding park is said to be the largest urban park in the nation. On the opposite side of the running water there is a pleasant walking trail which leads along the streambed for slightly over a half mile.

Mission Valley

El Camino Real (1789)

10818 San Diego Mission Road, San Diego 92108
Information Sources: 281-8449

Thomas Guide Pg.1249, H/7

El Camino Real, *The Royal Road*, was the connecting link between 21 Franciscan Missions of the Pacific Coast which were spaced out to be one day's horseback ride apart. In later years the original horse trail became the route of stage lines and is generally followed by remnants of U.S. Highway 101.

Importance of the mission route was emphasized when "official" markers in the form of copper/bronze bells were placed along Highway 101. On each bell was cast the legend *El Camino Real 1789-1806*. All the originals have been removed either to museums or by theft. Those pictured are replicas located at Mission San Diego de Alcala which was the first mission of the chain and southern terminus of the Camino. A portion of the original routing of *El Camino Real* is shown on page 1023, E/3 of the *Thomas Guide*.

Mission Valley

La Playa Trail (1770-1870)

10818 San Diego Mission Road, San Diego 92108
Information Sources: 281-8449

Thomas Guide Pg.1249, H/7

The legend on this tiny monument above the parking lot wall of Mission San Diego de Alcala records the former existence of *The oldest commercial trail in the Western United States.*

In the late 1790s and well into the 1800s La Playa was a shipping village on San Diego Bay in the area of Shelter Island Drive and Rosecrans Street. It was to here that ox carts traveled the La Playa Trail from inland ranches with their hides for shipment to Europe. In later years there was an adjacent rendering station which reduced whale meat to oil. Affluent La Playa residents moved inland as soon as they could afford it to escape the noisome commercial activity.

Mission Valley

Mother of the Missions (1769)

10818 San Diego Mission Road, San Diego 92108
Information Sources: 281-8449

Thomas Guide Pg.1249, G/7

This Mission church is at the second location of California's first Mission which was founded on July 16, 1769, on what is now known as Presidio Hill above Old Town San Diego. The present Mission, relocated here in 1774, is considered the first of the 21 missions of California. At one time this Mission controlled 50,000 acres of cultivated land. Later it was damaged by an earthquake, given to a Mexican national during the secularization of churches, used as a U.S.Cavalry post from 1846-1862 then returned to the Church by President Abraham Lincoln.

Moreno

Handicapped Accessible Park

Wildcat Canyon Road, Moreno 92040
Information Sources: 694-3049

Thomas Guide Pg.1212, D/7

This unique park, a gift to the County by Louis A. Stelzer, is over 300 acres of trails, picnic areas and viewpoints most of which are accessible by wheelchairs.

It is said to have been at one time a Kumeyaay Indian campsite which after County acceptance in 1971 was opened for public use in 1983. There are two main trails. One is a thirty-minute walk, the other takes about an hour. Marked paths lead to two viewpoints: Kumeyaay Promontory and Stelzer Ridge Summit.

National City

Brick Row (1887)

922 A Avenue, National City 91950
Information Sources: 477-9339

Thomas Guide Pg.1309, H/2

In 1887 these ten row-houses were built for a total of $30,000. Each unit is separated from its neighbor by an interlocking twelve-inch wall for privacy and strength. They were well finished homes with a butler's pantry and two fireplaces downstairs, and oak banisters and stairs leading to the four upstairs bedrooms. Setting of the bricks involved attention to artistic treatments including angled courses for the second storey and ornamental brick chimneys of which only a few remain. The front porch, which runs the length of the block-long building, has sectional divisions to separate the units each of which has an enclosed back yard.

The "Row" was built by National City founder Frank Kimball as housing for executives of the Santa Fe Railway which at that time was located in National City where the first west coast transcontinental railroad depot was located. After a few years in National City the Santa Fe moved its offices and terminal north to San Diego where it maintains a presence today.

Each of the houses is privately owned under protective restrictions which insure maintenance of the site in its original condition. The "Row" is registered in the National Register of Historic Places and is considered an important feature of National City's Heritage Square. There are four carefully preserved historic homes opposite the "Row" one of which was the Frank Kimball residence of 1868 (below) now owned by National City and open to the public as a Museum.

National City

Goesno Place

1000 Block of 32nd Street, National City 91950
Information Sources: 336-4290

Thomas Guide Pg.1309, G/5

This is the genuine Goesno Place along the east edge of National City's "Red" Pepper Park at the south end of Tidelands Avenue where there is a large parking lot and boat launching ramps for entry into San Diego Bay. There are no longer street signs for this one block which is the most imaginatively named street in San Diego. The 32nd Street near end is gated while the far end terminates by a restroom on banks of the Sweetwater River outfall. In effect, it goes no place.

National City

Transcontinental RR Station (1886)

900 West 23rd Street, National City 91950
Information Sources: 477-3451

Thomas Guide Pg.1309, G/3

This is the only original transcontinental terminus depot remaining in the United States. It was constructed in April of 1886 for use by the Santa Fe Transcontinental Railroad which terminated its cross-country traffic in National City. The track right-of-way has been used by the Coronado Belt-Line, National City and Otay, and Santa Fe railroads. It now benefits infrequent freight services.

Oak Grove

Civil War Barracks/Hospital (1861)

Post Mile 49.3 on HIghway 79, Oak Grove 92536
Information Sources: California Landmark *Thomas Guide Pg.409, H/5*

This Butterfield Stage Station was in operation from 1858 to 1861 at which time the Army took over the station buildings for use as a military hospital. During the Civil War members of the 1st California Volunteers were garrisoned here in 1861 as guards for stages and freight services between St.Louis and California. The post was named Camp Wright to honor Brigadier General George Wright who commanded the Pacific Department of the U.S.Army.

Both Camp Wright and the stage station were abandoned in late 1866.

Ocean Beach

Street of Tiles

Newport Avenue, Ocean Beach 92107
Information Sources: 224-4906 *Thomas Guide Pg.1267, J/6*

When the citizens of Ocean Beach wanted to improve their main street they raised money by selling tiles. Newport Avenue east of the beach carries hundreds of messages such as; *Sweet Angel, Herm & Me Fell in Love in OB...Lifeguard Loves 1945 Clarine Irene...The Pirate Loves His Wench...Michelle & Byron Out of Nothing at All 5-16-82...Fun Work OB Strand Gang Lee-Darryl-Bob...We Love OB, Phil Susan and Screamer...OB Centennial 1887-1987.*

Ocean Fishing

Fishing Piers

Oceanside to Imperial Beach, San Diego County
Information Sources: Noted

Thomas Guide Pg.Noted

Saltwater fishing in San Diego is a welcome relaxation. Bait shops offer rental hooks, lines and sinkers while many restaurants and recreational facilities adjoin the six piers: And there are 120 miles of fine beaches for surf fishing.

From north to south, the first site is a 2000-foot pier in Oceanside (above) with a restaurant at the seaward end and a bait shop for equipment. It is located at the end of 3rd Street (*Thomas 1105, J/1*). Further south in Pacific Beach is Crystal Pier which is unique for its overwater motel. There is a bait shop and fast-food nearby. The 700-foot pier is located at the end of Garnet Avenue (*Thomas 1247, H/6*). A major fishing pier is the T-shaped extension in Ocean Beach. It is almost 2000-feet long and has a bait shop and restaurant. It is located at the end of Niagara Street by a tiny parking lot (*Thomas 1267, H/6*). A lightly used facility near downtown San Diego is the Embarcadero Park Fishing Pier (below). It extends a short distance into waters of San Diego Bay. There is parking and a snack bar (*Thomas 1089, A/4*). Another bay-fishing pier is located on Harbor Island (*Thomas 1288, C/4*). Further south off Evergreen Avenue in Imperial Beach is a fine pier with a snack bar and bait shop (*Thomas 1349, E/1*).

Oceanside

Audubon Nature Center

2202 South Hill Street, Oceanside 92054
Information Sources: 439-2473

Thomas Guide Pg.1106, D/4

A coastal wetlands habitat in North San Diego County along shores of the lovely Buena Vista Lagoon is where a wide variety of natural history experiences may be enjoyed along a short trail bordered with native plants. In addition to views of the Lagoon and its bird life there is the potential (while walking) to discover animal tracks which represent the passage of nocturnal wild life on the same path.

Field trips are offered by the Audubon Society separately and in connection with monthly lectures. Special programs are scheduled for children and groups are encouraged to make reservations for selected tours. An unusual monthly event is a bird count of feathered residents of the Buena Vista Lagoon.

Oceanside

Surf Museum

308 North Pacific Street, Oceanside 92054
Information Sources: 721-6876

Thomas Guide Pg.1105, J/1

The California Surf Museum is a San Diego unique and there's no admission fee.

Inside the roughly finished structure is a mind-boggling display of surfboards ranging from solid wood skull-busters of the early days to new lightweight plastic speedsters representing the cutting edge of today's surfing art. Photographs, paintings and videos of world-famous surfing sites vie with images of record-holding competition surfers. The history and the future of the water sport is preserved in this untypical California exclusive.

Oceanside

Welcoming Arches

Hill Street at Goodland Drive, Oceanside 92054
Information Sources: 722-1534

Thomas Guide Pg.1085, J/6

The arches and included "Welcome Bell" are civic displays intended to welcome travelers to Oceanside. Unfortunately the display is almost hidden by extensive landscaping on the ocean side of Interstate 5 where traffic moves rapidly.

The structure is sited on the east side of Hill Street between Monterey and Goodland Drives. It was an Oceanside Chamber of Commerce project. An attached plaque reads *The Welcoming Arches were conceived from a wish that Oceanside's visitors receive a welcome reflecting the beauty, bounty and heritage of this area. Realizing where there is privilege there is also obligation, this entrance edifice was built by the voluntary generosity of the people of Oceanside. S/S: Lorraine Shaffer.*

In January of 1983 the Oceanside Rotary club added the "Welcome Bell" as its supportive share of the project.

Old Town

Court House (1850)

2635 San Diego Avenue, Old Town San Diego 92110
Information Sources: 220-5422

Thomas Guide Pg.1268, F/5

What appears to be a carefully restored small brick house in Old Town San Diego was the Court House when San Diego incorporated as California's first city on March 27, 1850. It has also been described as the heart of San Diego's first Anglo-American Civic Center and for a while was used as the City Hall.

Old Town

El Campo Santo Cemetery (1849)

San Diego Avenue at Aristo Avenue, Old Town San Diego 92110
Information Sources: 220-5422 *Thomas Guide Pg.1268, F/5*

El Campo Santo Cemetery in Old Town is a rewarding visit although it has been changed drastically since its early days as a plot of ground in which a known 447 burials were placed in random graves within and without its boundaries. The "Holy Field" Catholic cemetery was used from about 1849 to 1890 which is later than the opening of Calvary Cemetery under what is now Pioneer Park.

Around 1930 when Old Town began to grow El Campo's limits were moved inward which left a number of random graves outside the changed boundaries. Many of these graves are now under paved streets or sidewalks and have been recently marked. There are said to be 17 under San Diego Avenue and thirteen graves under Linwood Street. Most markers within the cemetery are more symbolic than representative of the burial site. There are said to be ten mass graves with no record to explain the graves'existence or individuals involved.

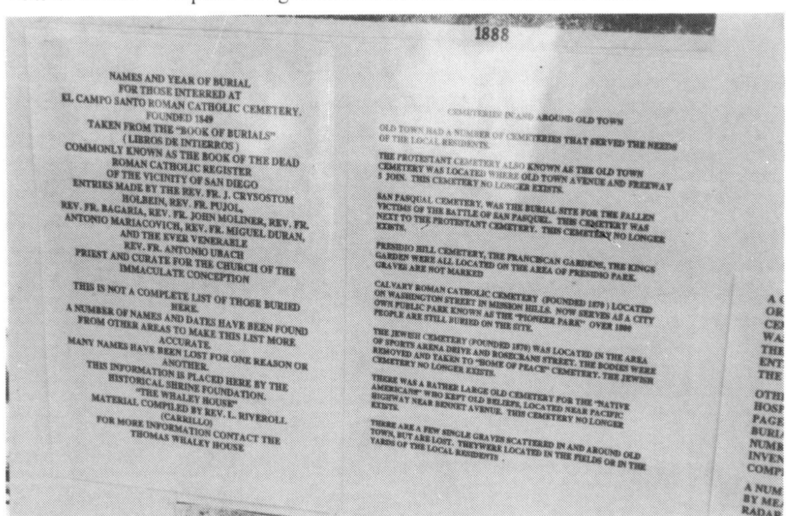

Old Town

First Public School (1865)

3966 Mason Street, Old Town San Diego 92110
Information Sources: 220-5422 *Thomas Guide Pg.1268, F/5*

Known as the Mason Street School this building was constructed without plans by volunteer labor using lumber salvaged from derelict structures. A local blacksmith, Frank Parsons, is credited with shingling the roof. It was Southern California's first publicly owned schoolhouse and served an area of about 15,000 square miles. An early teacher, Mary Chase Walker from San Francisco, was paid $65 a month. A bucket held drinking water and two outdoor privies served teacher and students. The school was closed in 1872. (Worth a visit!)

Old Town

Ghost of The Whaley House (1882)

2482 San Diego Avenue, Old Town San Diego 92110
Information Sources: 298-2482 *Thomas Guide Pg.1268, F/5*

In 1882 "Yankee" Jim Robinson was hanged near the Whaley House and ever since his ghost has protested Jim's innocence by moving furniture, thumping on walls and making his eerie presence known with random spooking events.

The House, built in 1856-57, was San Diego's first brick residence constructed of locally manufactured bricks. It is now said to be the oldest brick structure in Southern California. From 1869 to 1874 it was the County Courthouse. Later two of the four upstairs bedrooms were leased to "The Tanner Troupe" of actors that provided theatrical entertainment in San Diego County. It has been restored with remarkable accuracy and is decorated with authentic furnishings.

Old Town

Kearney Trail Terminus (1846)

On the Plaza, Old Town San Diego 92110
Information Sources: 220-5422 *Thomas Guide Pg.1268, F/5*

On December 6, 1846, a detachment of U.S.Dragoons under the command of General Stephen W. Kearney suffered severe losses inflicted by native California Lancers during the battle of San Pasqual. The Dragoons hurried five miles toward San Diego and camped at what is now known as "Mule Hill." Californian's surrounded the Dragoons who had to kill their mules for food and in so doing gave the hill its name. The U.S. troops were rescued by reinforcements from San Diego and this Old Town monument commemorates their safe arrival on December 12th.

Old Town

Old Town San Diego (ca.1790)

4002 Wallace Street, Old Town San Diego 92110
Information Sources: 220-5422 *Thomas Guide Pg.1268, F/5*

There's no secret to Old Town San Diego but the numerous sights with bits and pieces of historic trivia are well worth the time of exploration. Here you will now find buildings dating from 1827 when El Pueblo de San Diego was a sleeping Mexican village influenced by the military presence on Presidio Hill.

San Diego was declared California's first incorporated city on March 27, 1850 when, for the most part, what is now Old Town was the central portion of the community. Guided and self-guided tours begin at State Park offices on the north-west side of the Plaza which is surrounded by food and tourist services.

Old Town

Peace Memorial

Twiggs and San Diego Avenue, Old Town San Diego 92110
Information Sources: 220-5422 *Thomas Guide Pg.1268, F/5*

The Peace Memorial was installed by members of the local Vietnam Veterans organizations. On Memorial Day and at other selected times veterans assemble here for a sympathetic reading of names listed on the tablets.

Old Town

Ramona's Marriage Place (1829)

On the Plaza, Old Town San Diego 92110
Information Sources: 220-5422 *Thomas Guide Pg.1268, F/5*

Though it was known for many years as "Ramona's Marriage Place" as the result of a popular book, this carefully restored adobe is properly identified as La Casa de Estudillo. As such it was the social and political center of early San Diego.

Capitan Jose Maria Estudillo ordered construction of his home in 1829 on land granted him for service as commander of the San Diego Presidio. Estudillo died in 1830 but his son Jose Antonio completed the structure. Kumeyaay Indians worked on the project which made use of log rafters roofed by mats and fired-clay tiles. Bricks for the adobe walls were sun-baked. In one area there are floor tiles from the Mission Dam. Deterioration, obvious by the 1880s, was halted in 1908 when the adobe was completely restored as a visitor attraction. Later it became a part of the California State Park system and was restored again, this time as a museum of Estudillo family life and the early residents of Old Town San Diego.

Olivenhain

Bachelor's Shanty (1884-85)

Rancho Santa Fe Road at 7th Street, Olivenhain 92024
Information Sources: 632-9711 *Thomas Guide Pg.1147, J/7*

Not all colonists arriving in Olivenhain were married and the Colony built a number of these Bachelors' Shanties to house single men and men who were married but awaiting their family. This remaining example is held together by square nails, has clippings from tin cans nailed over the many knotholes and seems to show a few random bullet holes. It was relocated here.

Olivenhain

Colony Meeting Hall (1894)

Rancho Santa Fe Road at 7th Street, Olivenhain 92024
Information Sources: 632-9711 *Thomas Guide Pg.1147, J/7*

The 50 German families who settled Olivenhain are said to have volunteered the labor, and much of the material, to built this community hall for $6.

Originally the redwood structure was one large room with benches along the sides and a kitchen area in the rear. It was used for community meetings and parties. It has been carefully maintained in the original condition and is usually available for weddings and private social events.

Olivenhain **Germania Hotel (1895)**

Rancho Santa Fe Road at 7th Street, Olivenhain 92024
Information Sources: 632-9711 *Thomas Guide Pg.1147, J/7*

This two-storey structure was originally the home of Herman Baecht. It contains about 1600 square feet and is constructed of redwood planking to contain seven bedrooms and two living rooms. The building is described as "solidly constructed" of knot-free redwood in the best of German craftsmanship. It has been relocated and preserved in the same parklike surroundings as the Lickert Bachelor Shanty and the Olivenhain Community Hall.

It was named the Germania Hotel because Mrs. Baecht accepted borders and many original Olivenhain settlers lived here until their farm homes were ready for occupancy. Otherwise it was not a typical hotel because there was little access to water and the location was distant from the railroad and county stage lines. It is reported that colony families by the name of Guntner, Wallenstein, Cole and Winter were among those resident in the Germania.

Behind it is a relatively modern concrete dance floor built by the Town Council. Donors to the building fund were encouraged to inscribe their messages in fresh concrete around the perimeter. It appears to have been completed in 1972.

Otay Mesa

Air Wing Memorial (1883)

3560 Palm Avenue, San Diego 92154
Information Sources: 236-6661

Thomas Guide Pg.1350, D/1

Glider flights were made on this site in 1883 by John Joseph Montgomery, a school teacher who built several heavier-than-air craft decades before the Wright brothers. The airplane wing is the community's tribute to his pioneering talents.

Pacific Beach

Crystal Pier Motor Hotel

4500 Ocean Boulevard, Pacific Beach 92109
Information Sources: 483-6983

Thomas Guide Pg.1247, H/6

Though the pier is short, this is one of of the more interesting sites in San Diego and the only place to overnight above the ocean in motel cabins.

The Crystal Pier Motor Hotel and surrounding snack and gift shops are a throwback to 1927 when the pier was opened with a large ballroom at the end. In 1983 a major storm struck the coast and subtracted about 300 feet of the pier and its structures leaving only the stub which welcomes thousands of visitors annually.

Pacific Beach

Dolphins for Children

4000 Fanuel Street, San Diego 92109
Information Sources: 221-8899

Thomas Guide Pg.1247, J/7

In this tiny park at the end of Fanuel Street on the sands of Mission Bay is a school of happy dolphins for children to enjoy and explore.

Pacific Seashores

Tidepools

Oceanside to Imperial Beach, San Diego County
Information Sources: Noted

Thomas Guide Pg Noted

Tidepooling is a way of life for many San Diegans and a recreational activity that requires only an interest in ocean lore, tired tennis shoes and warm clothes.

One of the best places to learn is Ranger-led tidepooling in Cabrillo National Monument. With that bit of background you can then explore during low tide at False Point (La Jolla, *Thomas 1247, G/4*) at the end of Linda Way off Sea Ridge. Another area is South Cardiff State Beach (*Thomas 1126, H/6*) and below Sea Cliff (Swami's) Park (*Thomas 1167, C/1*). South of the Ocean Beach Pier at the foot of Narragansett Avenue (*Thomas 1267, H/6)* there is a small tidepool.

Pala

Cupa Cultural Center

Pala-Temecula Road, Pala 92059
Information Sources: 742-1590

Thomas Guide Pg.1029, H/4

The Pala Indian Reservation contains a valuable historic resource known as The Cupa Cultural Center. Within its walls are a library of Indian-based research material, a fine museum with classrooms and work areas for the instruction and preservation of Indian crafts. The Center is owned and managed by native California Indians residing on the Pala Reservation. Their books, tapes and language classes serve to keep alive the heritage of the Indian past.

Until 1903 the Cupenos lived in the village of Kupa by what is now known as Warner Hot Springs. They were evicted from their homes and taken to Pala which was a Luiseno village. Concurrently the Pala Indian Reservation was established on 3500 acres of Federal land.

Pala
Pala Mission Road, Pala 92059
Information Sources: 742-3317

Oldest Active Church (1816)

Thomas Guide Pg.1029, J/4

Mission San Antonio de Pala, in San Diego's North County, is regarded as the area's oldest continually serving church. It was founded in 1816 as a subsidiary of Mission San Luis Rey de Francia near Oceanside. Franciscan Friars, who staff the Pala Mission, say it has the distinction of being the only Mission in California that has ministered continually to needs of the Indians for whom it was originally built.

The campanile is known for its distinctive architecture and construction separate from the mission quadrangle. The two original bells have been used since the founding in 1816. Original roof tiles cover the chapel and the adjacent cemetery includes burials dating from the founding era.

Palm City

Salt Ponds (1922)

Bay Boulevard at Belle Street, Palm City 92154
Information Sources: 566-6600

Thomas Guide Pg.1330, A/4

An almost forgotten industry, the reclamation of salt from evaporated sea water, is alive and well in the Western Salt Works at the southern end of San Diego Bay.

Since 1922 this facility has been producing kiln-dried sea salt which is marketed for water softening and gourmet food seasoning. Visitors are not allowed in the plant but by parking on nearby Bay Boulevard it is possible to view the huge complex of ponds and watch bulldozers scraping salt for transport to the adjacent mill. Rusty rails between Bay Boulevard and Western Salt were originally laid in 1888 for the Coronado Steam Railroad which provided passenger and freight transportation between the City of San Diego and the Hotel Del Coronado. Now they are reported to be a portion of the San Diego and Arizona Eastern Railroad.

Palomar Mountain

Boucher Hill Lookout

County S-7 to State Park Road, Palomar Mountain 92060
Information Sources: 742-3462 *Thomas Guide Pg.409, G/7*

A most spectacular viewpoint, and one that's easy to reach, is the Boucher Hill Lookout owned by the California Department of Forestry on Palomar Mountain. It is accessed by driving direct ahead after passing the State Park entry kiosk. Original use was as a fire lookout offering full circle observation of much of San Diego's forest land. The lookout is now closed but there are picnic benches and the fantastic view. Notice the snow ladder on the roof for emergency exit from the tower if an unexpected snowstorm blocks the ground level door.

Palomar Mountain

Civilian Conservation Corps Site

County S-7 to State Park Road, Palomar Mountain 92060
Information Sources: 742-3462 *Thomas Guide Pg.409, G/7*

Only a few yards past the entry kiosk into Palomar Mountain State Park you'll find this marble plate (1987) on the left side of the roadway. The inscription reads: *Dedicated to all who served here on Palomar Mountain and to the three million who served in the CCC nationwide, 1933-1942. The CCC still lives in spirit. It has left its monuments in the preservation and purification of the land, the water, the forests and the young men of America.*

Palomar Mountain

Nate Harrison Toll Road

County S-7 to State Park Road, Palomar Mountain 92060
Information Sources: 742-3462 *Thomas Guide Pg.409, G/7*

Local history has it that a freed black slave, Nate Harrison, built a toll road from the Pauma Valley up to the trees of Palomar Mountain. The monument to his life (above) is located near where Harrison lived. As wagons groaned their way up the steep grade he is said to have always greeted teamsters with fresh cool water from the nearby spring...and probably collected his toll fee at the same time.

In 1921, when the monument was built, there was an engraved bronze plaque which read: *Nathan Harrison's spring. Brought here a slave about 1848, died October 10, 1920, aged 101 years. A man's a man for a 'that'.*

However it is known that Nate Harrison was much younger when he died. An 1894 voter registration form shows his age as 61 and his birthplace as Kentucky where it is believed he was born a slave. There are differing versions of his gaining freedom and it is said a portion of his slavery was served in California.

Palomar Mountain

Observatory (1948)

35899 Canfield Road/County S-6, Palomar Mountain 92060
Information Sources: 742-2119 *Thomas Guide Pg.409, G/6*

Though it took 20 years from start to finish, the Palomar Observatory and its 200-inch Hale Telescope has been remarkably productive.

In 1928 an agency of the Rockefeller Foundation awarded a grant to Pasadena's CalTech for the telescope. A site was found and techniques were developed for casting the 20-ton glass disk in 1934. The outbreak of war in 1941 halted construction and delayed polishing of the mirror. It was 1947 before the mirror was trucked to Palomar Mountain and the Observatory opened in 1948. On site is a small museum, gift shop and information on visits to the Observatory.

Pauma Valley

Indian Water Park

Hiway 76 & Sengme Oaks Road, San Diego County 97082
Information Sources: 742-1921 *Thomas Guide Pg.409, G/8*

In beautifully remote Pauma Valley the La Jolla Band of Mission Indians have installed a Water Park with RV sites and a splendid camping area. The Park includes a variety of water sport facilities, picnic shelters and is in the middle of a fine network of hiking and walking trails. Many San Diego residents use the Park as an all-day respite from the bustle of city life.

There is another water park in the City of Vista (*Thomas Pg.1087*) at 161 Recreation Drive. Telephone 940-9283 for information.

Point Loma

Coast Guard Lighthouse (1891)

Cabrillo Road, San Diego 92106
Information Sources: 557-6556

Thomas Guide Pg.1308, A/3

When the first lighthouse on the higher ground of Point Loma was closed in 1891, because it was so far above the frequent coastal fog that mariners could seldom see the light, this larger installation was opened near sea level.

As a Coast Guard installation there are living quarters for the staff controlling the Point Loma Light and its numerous water-level fog horns delimiting San Diego Bay entrance channels.

Point Loma

Coastal Defense Searchlights (1918)

Bayside Trail, Cabrillo National Pk. 92106
Information Sources: 557-5450

Thomas Guide Pg.1308, A/2

During WW I the U.S.Army installed heavy artillery and supporting equipment in bunkers on Point Loma. On the Bayside Trail are two accessible sites. The nearest held a 60-inch searchlight mounted on train wheels to reach the cliffside on tracks which remain at the bottom of the door. In the distance is the bunker which held a gasoline-powered generator to energize the searchlight. Poking its light tower above the hilltop on the right is the old Point Loma Lighthouse of 1854.

Point Loma

National Cemetery (1934)

Cabrillo Memorial Drive, San Diego 92106
Information Sources: 553-2084

Thomas Guide Pg.1288, A/7

Nearly 50,000 of the nation's honored dead are buried in the Fort Rosecrans National Cemetery. The granite boulder in the foreground marks the burial site of 17 soldiers and a civilian who died during the Battle of San Pasqual. The 75-foot obelisk is "The Bennington Monument" commemorating an explosion on the U.S.S.Bennington in 1905 which killed an officer, 65 crewmen and injured others.

Point Loma

Point Loma Lighthouse (1854)

Cabrillo Memorial Drive, Point Loma 92106
Information Sources: 557-5450

Thomas Guide Pg.1308, A/2

Floor tiles from a ruined Spanish fort and sandstone carved from supporting hills were used in construction of this reminder of sailing ships and oil lamps. The Old Point Loma Lighthouse is 422 feet above sea level, a location which eventually proved to be its undoing. High fog and low clouds often obscured the light beam and in 1891 the facility was closed.

First use of the lighthouse was on November 15, 1855, a year after construction was completed. The delay was caused by the slow delivery of illumination equipment and a five-foot fresnel lens which had been ordered from French makers. The thick-walled building is protected by a rolled tin roof around the circular brick tower which houses the oil lamp and its projection equipment.

Point Loma

WW II Observation Bunker

At Old Point Loma Lighthouse, Cabrillo National Pk. 92106
Information Sources: 557-5450 *Thomas Guide Pg.1308, A/2*

During WW II this bunker was built on the outer edge of the highest point on Point Loma. It was used to monitor traffic in and out of San Diego Bay as well as provide radio communications through equipment sited in the Old Point Loma Lighthouse. This bunker can best be viewed while walking down the Bayside Trail

Poway

Big Train in Little Park

14114 Midland Road, Poway 92064
Information Sources: 679-8587 *Thomas Guide Pg.1190, F/2*

Old Poway Park is host to one of the shortest and most unique rail lines in the nation. About a half mile of standard gauge railroad circles though a small urban park for the benefit of a gasoline-powered track inspection car, a tiny steam locomotive and an antique street railway car being modified for use on the park's shortline railroad.

All of which makes Old Poway Park a convenient place to view and ride a display of historic railroad equipment amid suburban country-side surroundings.

Presidio Park

Fort Stockton Site (1847)

Presidio Drive at Cosoy Way, Old Town San Diego 92110
Information Sources: 692-4918 *Thomas Guide Pg.1268, F/4*

From 1838 to 1848 this hilltop area was a fortified stockade to protect the collection of adobes located in what is now known as Old Town San Diego.

Carlos Carrillo briefly fortified the area in 1838. A decade later, from July to November of 1846, it was Fort Dupont and occupied by American troops who held it and the Old Town area in the name of the United States. The Californians counterattacked and briefly held both San Diego and the fort. Shortly thereafter an augmented force of American soldiers were successful in retaking the area at which time they named it Fort Stockton. From this hilltop the Americans conducted their military campaign which eventually concluded the war in 1847. The famous Mormon Battalion was stationed here before being transferred north. As a military post Fort Stockton was abandoned September 28, 1848.

Presidio Park Fr. Francisco Palau Memorial (1929)

Presidio Drive at Cosoy Way, Old Town San Diego 92110
Information Sources: 297-3258 *Thomas Guide Pg.1268, F/4*

On July 13, 1929, the Native Daughters of the Golden West dedicated this tree to the memory of Fr. Francisco Palou who was the biographer of Fr. Serra founder of the California Mission Chain. It is from Fr. Palou that we have background on the Missions as Fr. Serra was busier building Missions than writing about them. The tree is located near the site of Fort Stockton on Presidio hill.

Presidio Park Lucy's Monument

Presidio Drive by Serra Museum, Old Town San Diego 92110
Information Sources: 297-3258 *Thomas Guide Pg.1268, F/4*

The legends of Presidio Park include the drinking bowl and ghost of Lucy, a white deer who at one time roamed in the surrounding Mission Valley hills.

According to Gail White's book *Haunted San Diego* "The best times to experience Lucy are at twilight and the early morning hours." She is said to have been born in the San Diego Zoo, was sold to a private owner, escaped and lived happily in the area for nearly ten years. Though she had become a community pet, worry-warts decided she should be relocated. When she was tranquilized the medication caused a heart attack and Lucy became a happy memory.

Her drinking fountain is easily found on the peak of Inspiration Point. Stand in the doorway of the Serra Museum and face south along the long entry porch. Direct ahead is a small hill on which Lucy's fountain remains. The base has footprints of animals, including Lucy's, embedded in the concrete. Vandals have destroyed a portion of the bowl which no longer is kept full of water.

Presidio Park

Mounted Charro (1970)

Cosoy Way, Old Town San Diego 92110
Information Sources: 692-4918

Thomas Guide Pg.1268, F/4

This fine work was a gift from the people of Mexico to the City of San Diego in 1969 on what was considered the City's 200th birthday. It was done by Join Fernando Olaquibel. Unfortunately the statue didn't arrive in town until 1970.

Accordingly the bronze plaque on the base reads *Donado a la Ciudad de San Diego Por El Senor Licenciado Gustavo Diaz Ordaz Presidente de la Republica Mexicana Noviembre de 1970.*

Ramona

Castle, Amy Strong's (1916-21)

Mount Woodson Way, Ramona 92065
Information Sources: Gate Guard

Thomas Guide Pg.1171, F/3

From 1916 to 1921 Amy Strong directed construction of this 27-room, 12,000 square-foot, "Castle" which remains as solid as the day it was built. Ms. Strong was a well-off dressmaker who served the influential families of San Diego for about 20 years at the turn of the century during which time she purchased 380 acres in the Mount Woodson area for her "farm" and home site.

Inside are Indian carvings, four fireplaces and and a sundial on the dining room ceiling. During the holiday season over 32,000 lights are hung to outline the building and illuminate the roof with a "Merry Xmas" greeting. A life-size nativity setting is frequently installed on the front lawn.

Ramona

Fly-Bye Mail Box

Highway 67 and Air Mail Lane, Ramona 92065
Information Sources: 789-1220

Thomas Guide Pg.1171, J/3

For over ten years the mail box above the car has entertained passers-by along the main San Diego/Ramona highway. The post office reports that mail service is not provided due to the shortage of delivery personnel. Accidents have activated volunteered repairs and a road crew reset the post during pavement widening.

Ramona

Grange Hall (1895)

215 Seventh Street, Ramona 92065
Information Sources: 789-7644

Thomas Guide Pg.1152, G/5

This tiny structure was built in 1895 for a rural department store then located at 733 Main Street. In 1924 it was moved to the present site for use by Ramona Grange # 2 which designation was later changed to # 632 as one of the largest such farm groups in San Diego County. It is presently occupied by a church.

Rolando — Stairclimbers' Delight

X Lot Parking Area, SD State Univ., San Diego 92115
Information Sources: 594-6871 — *Thomas Guide Pg.1270, B/1*

Wandering up the hillside from the lower right to the upper left is one of the longer stairways in San Diego. Over 150 steps for those SDSU students who exercise from the parking area known as "X Lot." Kooperman's *San Diego Trivia 2* tells of a stairway with nearly 250 steps on Mount Nebo but reports it is hard to find.

San Diego County — Dog Beaches

Coastal Shores, Various locations
Information Sources: Noted — *Thomas Guide Pg.Noted*

The happiest canines in the County are those whose masters take them to either the Ocean Beach or Del Mar dog beach areas. At the north end of Ocean Beach by the San Diego River jetty is this special area (*Thomas 1267, J/5*) which merits a "Watch where you step" caution. A similar area by Del Mar Shores Beach Park, west of the Del Mar Race Track (*Thomas 1187, E/2*), is also open for running household pets and to exercise race horses in the ocean during the Del Mar season.

San Diego County

Free Railroad Station(1911)

Coast Boulevard at 15th Street, Del Mar 92014
Information Sources: 481-0114 *Thomas Guide Pg.1187, F/4*

Del Mar developer William Kerckhoff was not happy with the Santa Fe Railroad's traditional wooden stations. He built this handsome brick structure and gave it to the railroad in return for a promise they would always provide passenger service to Del Mar. A planned commuter rail service could eliminate the Amtrak stop.

San Diego County

Horse-Rings in Street Curbs

Various locations, San Diego
Information Sources: Noted *Thomas Guide Pg.Noted*

San Diego's somewhat rural heritage is shown in a number of areas where horse rings and hitching-posts remain or were installed as a neighborhood feature.

There are said to be rings along the curbs of Columbia Street, between A and B Streets in Uptown San Diego (*Thomas 1289, A/2*) and along F Street between 4th and 5th Streets (*Thomas 1289, A/3*). There is a ring in the curb at 4636 Date Avenue (*Thomas 1270, H/3*) and a contemporary hitching post in front of 8447 Lemon Avenue (*Thomas 1271, A/2*) in the photo above.

San Diego County
In all communities., Various
Information Sources: Noted

Information Centers

Thomas Guide Pg Noted

This fully staffed visitor's center (276-8200) is reached by taking the Clairemont Drive offramp from Interstate 5 (*Thomas Pg.1248, D/6*) and then turning toward Mission Bay and direction signs. There is another information center in Horton Plaza, one at 202 C Street, and an International Center (236-1212) at First Avenue and F Street (*Thomas Pg.1289, A/3*). For specific community information the best source is usually the Chamber of Commerce listed the local telephone book.

San Diego County
Various locations, San Diego
Information Sources: Noted

Jet Skiing

Thomas Guide Pg Noted

Jet-Skis have become as popular as wind-surfing boards in the San Diego area and Mission Bay waters surrounding Fiesta Island are the place to find them. Yellow pages of the telephone book list Jet-Ski rental agencies and sources of instruction for safe riding in waters surrounding San Diego.

Special areas that have been set aside for Jet-Skiing include separate sections for beginners and more experienced riders. To reach Fiesta Island leave Interstate 5 at Sea World Drive and turn toward the coast. In about one-quarter mile there is a right turn toward Fiesta Island which is followed rather quickly by a left turn onto the Island causeway. Traffic on Fiesta Island is one-way to the right and it is necessary to circle the entire island to find a predetermined parking lot.

San Diego County
Various locations, San Diego
Information Sources: Noted

Merry-Go-Rounds

Thomas Guide Pg.Noted

There's almost a half dozen fine carrousels in San Diego County. They include: Seaport Village, 874 Harbor Drive (*Thomas Pg.1288, J/4*) 234-6133; Balboa Park, 1549 El Prado (*Thomas Pg.1269, 7*) 239-0512; Chula Vista Shopping Center, Broadway and I Streets (*Thomas Pg.1310, A/7*); Parkway Plaza Shopping Center, 415 Parkway Plaza, El Cajon (*Thomas Pg.1251, F/4*) 579-9932; and a tiny one in Belmont Park, 3146 Mission Boulevard (*Thomas Pg.1267, H/3*) 488-0668.

San Diego County
Various locations, San Diego
Information Sources: Noted

Miniature Trains

Thomas Guide Pg.Noted

There's only a few miniature trains in San Diego, the best known being in Balboa Park (*Thomas Pg.1269, C/7*) 239-4748 and in the Antique Gas and Steam Engine Museum, 2040 North Santa Fe Avenue (*Thomas Pg.1087, F/2*), Vista, 941-1791. A few shopping centers and carnivals have small-fry trains on portable tracks.

San Diego County

Museums

88 Active Museums in San Diego,
Information Sources: 239-0512

Thomas Guide Pg Noted

In January 1993 the Museum of Contemporary Art opened this site at Kettner and Broadway, downtown, to exhibit a changing schedule of year-around showings. Balboa Park has The Automotive Museum, Museum of Man, San Diego Museum of Art, Timken Art Gallery, Natural History Museum, Fleet Science Center, Museum of Photographic Arts, San Diego Historical Society Archives and Aerospace Historical Center. In the County there is the Steam Museum (Vista), Chula Vista Nature Center and local museums of quality. There are nearly ninety museums described in Coda Publications book *Museums & Gardens of San Diego.*

San Diego County

Open Air Theaters

Various locations, San Diego
Information Sources: Noted

Thomas Guide Pg Noted

There are a number of open-air theaters in San Diego County, many of which are easily reached by public transportation. The best known is Starlight Bowl (544-7827) in Balboa Park (above) which maintains fine seasons of professional entertainment. Balboa Park also has free organ concerts every Sunday off the Prado in an open-air setting. Chula Vista's Memorial Park is the site of local programs provided by the Chula Vista Recreation Department (691-5071). There is a beach-front theater in Oceanside (966-4530), a hillside theater in Vista (724-6017) and another in Escondido's Kit Carson Park (432-4538).

San Diego County
Noted, La Jolla 92037
Information Sources: 236-7181

U-Turn Bridges

Thomas Guide Pg Noted

What may be a County record in creative road design is found in the hills behind La Jolla. Take Soledad Avenue off Torrey Pines Road (*Page 1227, F/6*) and turn right on Al Bahr Drive. In a few blocks you will pass under a bridge (above) then U-Turn back and pass over the same bridge. Make an immediate right on Crespo Drive (which wanders) and follow it to Castellano Road (*Page 1227, G/6*) on the right. Continue uphill on Castellano and you will pass a bridge (below) leading to Puente Drive as you make a descending U-Turn to the left under the same bridge. If you're a bit lost, continue ahead on Castellano to Hillside Drive then go left downhill back to Torrey Pines Road. Great homes with breathtaking ocean views.

San Diego County

Wilderness Camping

Camino San Ignacio off Highway 79, Warner Springs 92086
Information Sources: 782-3269 *Thomas Guide Pg.409, K/7*

This entrance gate leads to a wonderful wilderness area located in the largest Indian Reservation in San Diego County. It is also home to the highest peak; Hot Springs Mountain (6535 feet) with an abandoned fire lookout tower on top.

There are miles of walking and hiking trails ranging from easy to difficult. Plus routes for jeeping, cross-country skiing and mountain bicycling. The area is open all year with weather permitting. Camping is primitive though water and toilets are in the main campground. Permits and a modest fee are required. Los Coyotes is one of the few campgrounds which allows open fires.

San Luis Rey

Mission San Luis Rey (1798)

4050 Mission Avenue, San Luis Rey 92068
Information Sources: 757-3651 *Thomas Guide Pg.1086, H/2*

Known as "King of the Missions" this monument to Spanish colonization at one time controlled 27,000 head of cattle, 26,000 sheep and large agricultural holdings worked by the Mission's thousands of local Indian converts.

Large scale restoration has brought the Mission to a beauty that far exceeds its original form. It now serves as a parish church and a center for religious retreats and conferences. A museum has exhibits on the history of California missions and displays the deed of 1862 signed by Abraham Lincoln.

San Luis Rey

Oldest Pepper Tree (1830)

4050 Mission Avenue, San Luis Rey 92068
Information Sources: 757-3250

Thomas Guide Pg.1086, H/2

What is said to be the first pepper tree grown in California continues to enhance the friary garden area on the west side of Mission San Luis Rey de Francia. In the early years this same quadrangle was the site of Indian bullfighting entertainment.

The pepper tree was brought to California from Peru in 1830. It is at the largest of all California missions which was the 18th of the Pacific Coast chain when founded June 13, 1798 by Padre Lasuen. The church is said to have been the largest building in California until about 1845. Church walls are the major portions remaining from the original. Reconstruction of all buildings began in 1893.

San Marcos

One-Room Schoolhouses (1889-1910)

Various locations, San Marcos 92069
Information Sources: 744-9025

Thomas Guide Pg.1108, D/7

San Marcos is home to three one-room schoolhouses which is more than any other community in San Diego County. The 1910 Schoolhouse (above) was rescued from a vacant lot and restored at 1511 Grand Avenue by William Carroll. It has since been open to the public as a newspaper office, antique store and restaurant.

The Richland School (1889) is located at 885 Richland/Woodland Road (*Thomas Guide 1109, B/7*). It has been lovingly restored and is well maintained. The Twin Oaks Schoolhouse (1891) is located on North Deer Springs Road (*Thomas Guide 1108, J/1*). It has had routine maintenance but little restoration.

San Onofre

Atomic Energy Plant

Old Highway 101, San Onofre 92672
Information Sources: 714-368-2170

Thomas Guide Pg.1023, G/5

Nuclear Power from twin reactors is supplied to the Southern California power grid from this installation in San Onofre. It can be seen while driving north from San Diego on Interstate 5. To reach the front gate leave I-5 at Basilone Road and turn toward the ocean. Follow Old Highway 101 south toward San Onofre State Beach to the plant which is operated by the Southern California Edison Co. Group, family or individual tours may be arranged by telephoning 1-714-368-2170.

The Thomas Guide, Page 1023, shows a section of the original *El Camino Real* (1789-1826) along the north side of I-5.

San Pasqual

Battlefield at San Pasqual (1846)

15808 San Pasqual Valley Road, Escondido 92025
Information Sources: 489-0076

Thomas Guide Pg.1131, B/7

One of the bloodiest and most controversial military encounters during the Mexican-American War took place December 6 to 10, 1846, near this Visitor Center. The battle was between Californios led by Major Andres Pico and forces of the United States led by Brigadier General Stephen W. Kearney. The Californios inflicted heavy casualties on the Americans who buried their dead under a nearby tree. While fleeing to San Diego the Americans camped on a hilltop and were surrounded by the Californios. Without food, the U.S. troops resorted to eating their mules on what is known as "Mule Hill." On December 11 they were rescued by troops from San Diego. The 18 Americans killed at San Pasqual are buried in an honored mass grave at Fort Rosecrans on Point Loma.

San Ysidro

Border Crossing Rules

720 East San Ysidro Boulevard, San Ysidro 91932
Information Sources: 428-7311 *Thomas Guide Pg.1350, H/5*

The famous San Diego Trolley stops only a few feet from both the Mexican Border and a somewhat misplaced monument. The later is often taken to be location of the boundary line which is actually about 50 feet further south.

The informality of the nation's busiest border crossing belies the necessity of being able to prove one's citizenship. By all means carry documentation as to your identity, nativity and country of legal residence. Overseas visitors should carry their passport and certification of legal entry. If in doubt telephone the Border Patrol in San Ysidro for current regulations.

San Ysidro

Border Mounuments (1849)

Border Field State Park, San Diego 92173
Information Sources: 435-5184 *Thomas Guide Pg.1349, G/7*

A point from which to appreciate the boundary fence between Mexico and the United States is at this west-most boundary marker in Border Field State Park. The obelisk is fenced exactly in the middle. Past the fence on the Mexican side are food services and a bull ring This is Monument # 258 with Monument # 1 near Brownsville, Texas. Engraving reads *Initial point of Boundary between the United States and Mexico. Established by the joint commission October A.D. 1849 agreeably to the Treaty date at the City of Guadelupe Hidalgo February 2 A.D. 1848. John E. Weller U.S.Commission. Andrew S. Gray U.S.Surveyor.*

Santee

Polo Barn (1913)

9064 Edgemoor Drive, Santee 92071
Information Sources: 258-3001

Thomas Guide Pg.1231,E/6

Variously known as the "Polo Barn and the "Edgemoor Farm Barn" this unusual structure is said to be the only remaining example of a Dutch gambrel roof on a farm structure in San Diego County. It was completed in 1913 as the centerpiece of a major effort to raise polo ponies under ideal conditions. Barn floors were of cork to protect the pony's feet and nearby meadows were used as exercise fields.

Shelter Island

Bell of Friendship (1960)

Shelter Island Drive, San Diego 92106
Information Sources: 686-5470

Thomas Guide Pg.1288, B/4

At the tip of Shelter Island you'll find the Bell of Friendship presented to the people of San Diego on December 10, 1960, by the citizens of Yokohama, Japan, "As a symbol of eternal friendship." It's easy to find by turning right as you drive onto Shelter Island and following the Drive to its circular cul-de-sac.

Shelter Valley

Earthquake Valley

County Highway S-2 at 78, Shelter Valley 92036
Information Sources: 767-4684

Thomas Guide Pg.1138, C/6

Though residents prefer its adopted name of "Shelter Valley," a section of the Great Southern Overland Stage Route of 1849 passes through Earthquake Valley. The name stems from existence of the San Felipe Valley (Earthquake) Fault which lies along the valley floor. Two-mile-long Shelter Valley is south of the intersection of State Highway 78 and County Highway S-2 at Scissors Crossing, so named for its appearance on road maps of the area.

The mythical sign at this intersection of S-2 and Kickin (sic) Horse Trail is identified as "Histerical (sic) Monument of 1984." The sign's multi-line legend details wondrous events which could have happened but likely did not.

Silver Strand

Seals' Training Beach

U.S.Naval Amphibious Base, Coronado 92118
Information Sources: 437-2011

Thomas Guide Pg.1309, A/2

A training area for the Navy's famous underwater Seals is along the ocean side of the Silver Strand south of the Hotel Del Coronado.

Rigorous workouts along the beach include an ambulance for trainees who become incapacitated. Further south on property not open to the public are concrete bunkers and retired helicopters which are used during attack simulations. A portion of this installation may be seen from Silver Strand Boulevard.

Solana Beach

600 Stevens Avenue, Solana Beach 92075
Information Sources: 755-2998

Carved Boulder (1986)

Thomas Guide Pg.1187, G/1

"The Angels and The Children" is the name of this introspective work by Thomas Parker Emery who, spend three months carving on 25 tons of stone for this monument to the founding of Solana Beach in 1986. Emery remembers well that Mexican children brought him food in appreciation of his delight in their watching him work from sketches their parents had reviewed. Says Emery, "I wanted La Colonia Park to always have children...and angels to watch over them."

Solana Beach

100 Block South Cedros, Solana Beach 92075
Information Sources: 755-4775

Quonset Hut Lofts (1949)

Thomas Guide Pg.1167, E/7

This striking row of office buildings was constructed in 1949 to house the workshops of the Bill Jack Scientific Instrument Company which is said to have produced aerial reconnaissance cameras and specialized photographic equipment. An advantage to the "Quonset-type" second floor is the economy of construction in which the walls and roof are of self-supporting corrugated metal. Current renovation and upgrading of the structure has created an avant-garde shopping strip with many unusual retailers and services.

In the early days of Solana Beach this area of Cedros (Cedars) Avenue was a dirt road serving avocado growers and area farmers on their way to town.

Needle's Eye

Sunset Cliffs
Sunset Cliffs Boulevard at Hill St., San Diego 92107
Information Sources: 224-2708

Thomas Guide Pg.1287, H/2

Legend has it that in years past an eager surfer rode his board into the narrow slot in Sunset Cliffs which is now surrounded by a chain-link fence. Be that as it may, during periods of incoming tide it is a stimulating point from which to enjoy the ocean's force and wonder about the wisdom of threading the "Needle's Eye."

Earthquake Fault

Tecolate Canyon
East of Tecolate Park Entry, San Diego 92110
Information Sources: 490-0930

Thomas Guide Pg.1248, F/4

There's a clearly visible, and easily reached, earthquake fault just a few short miles from center-city San Diego.

The site is in Tecolate Park which is primarily a canyon wandering east of Interstate 5. Use the Tecolate Road offramp and turn inland. Follow the pavement about a mile to a cul-de-sac with Park offices on the right. To find the earthquake fault either ask for directions at the Park office or walk toward the fenced ballfield near the office. Between the office and ballfield is a paved path leading upward toward cliffs which are about 100 yards behind the office. Follow the path and continue past a second ballfield located on a slight rise. After passing the second ballfield you will be facing the fault on the cliff ahead.

The cliff face by the concrete drainage channel and to the right is speckled with cobblestones and a section of earth totally different from the sandstone cliff face on the left. These two distinct land masses have slipped from their original location and been forced upward to be visible as fault sections.

Torrey Pines

Black's (Nude) Beach

End of Torrey Pines Scenic Drive, La Jolla 92037
Information Sources: 755-2063

Thomas Guide Pg.1207, G/7

The entry to the Black's Beach area is a narrow cliff-hugging path to the left of the gliderport as you face the ocean. The shore south of this point toward La Jolla is a City of San Diego beach where nude bathing is outlawed. North toward Torrey Pines is Torrey Pines State Beach where, it is reported, nude bathing is tolerated. If in doubt inquire and bypass the embarrassment of doing what comes naturally but which may not be acceptable where you are.

Torrey Pines

Gliderport

End of Torrey Pines Scenic Drive, La Jolla 92037
Information Sources: 525-8281

Thomas Guide Pg.1207, H/7

This area was at one time a gliderport where sailplanes were launched aloft over the La Jolla cliffs onto a near constant breeze from the ocean.

Though still known as "The Gliderport" its primary current use is for parasailing where winged enthusiasts literally jump off cliffs which at their least are several hundred feet high. It's more than exciting to watch such antics.

Uptown San Diego

Gabriel On the Roof (1910)

2825 5th Avenue, San Diego Uptown 92103
Information Sources: 686-8700

Thomas Guide Pg.1289, A/2

When built in 1910 as the Park Place Methodist Episcopal Church this lovely structure was a keystone of religious activity in San Diego. By the mid-1970's the church moved on and the building was renovated for use as *The Abbey* social hall for dancing and dining. It was then that Gabriel was completed with genuine gold leaf and his home entered into the National Register of Historic Places.

Uptown SD

Priceless Fig Tree (1880)

350 Grape Street, San Diego 92101
Information Sources: 239-0512

Thomas Guide Pg.1289, A/1

This Moreton Bay Fig tree was designated as San Diego Historic Site 53 on a block that at one time was occupied by the Florence Hotel of 1884. As recorded in a survey of historic sites within the city, this tree was one of three in San Diego County in 1980. At that time its value was estimated to be between $110,000 and $140,000 based on rarity and size.

Vallecito **Butterfield Stage Station Site**

County S-2 at Post Mile 35, Vallecito 92036
Information Sources: 694-3049 *Thomas Guide Pg.430, C/2*

The Vallecito Stage Station on this site was originally built in 1852 at what was then described as "the edge of the great Colorado desert." It was also a stop-over for the first transcontinental mail route (The Jackass Mail) which operated from 1857 to 1859, for emigrant wagon trains and Butterfield stages.

A plaque inside the building records early uses of the water sources by area Indians, Spanish explorers in 1782, Mexican trail-breakers of 1826, Kit Carson in 1846, General Stephen Kearney (Kearny) and his Dragoons on the way to the Battle of San Pasqual in 1846, the Mormon Battalion in 1847 and stage passengers of Butterfield & Company of 1858-1861. The present structure (1934) is a "faithful" reproduction of the original and its walls are made of the same salt-grass bricks from material gathered in the area. Overnight campers are said to report hearing ghostly hoofbeats and stage noises during the dark hours and finding fresh wheel ruts and hoof marks in the morning.

Viejas Band
5000 Willows Road, Alpine 91901
Information Sources:

Bungee Jumping

Thomas Guide Pg.1235, A/5

It's not there any more but for over a year it was possible to Bungee-Jump off what was said to be the nation's tallest bungee tower. For about $100 one could walk to the end of the ramp, look over the edge at a tiny pool of water 210 feet below then take a deep breath and step or leap off into thin air and hope the rubber bungee cord was securely fastened at both ends: To the tower and the ankles. The distant location for an impulse sport and lack of business is said to have hastened the tower's removal to a new location in Long Beach near Los Angeles.

Vista

Adobe, Most Beautiful (1845)

640 Alta Vista Drive, Vista 92083
Information Sources: 945-4919

Thomas Guide Pg.1087, J/6

From an 1884 land grant of 1184 acres, Rancho Buena Vista eventually grew to 4269 acres of prime land in what is now the City of Vista. Today this lovely adobe of 1845 is sited on less than two acres of the original ranch.

The hacienda is said to have not suffered any major architectural alterations and its historic integrity has been well maintained. It is described as the "best-preserved and cared for" of the San Diego County ranchos. Interior furnishings and exterior artifacts are in keeping with the significance of this fine monument. It is owned by the City of Vista and open to the public.

Vista

Steam Engines

2040 North Santa Fe Avenue, Vista 92083
Information Sources: 941-1791

Thomas Guide Pg.1087, G/2

In the 40-acre Antique Gas & Steam Engine Museum are steam engines, gas engines and diesel engines from tiny washing-machine power to a mammoth Corliss steam engine considered to be the high point in development of stationary power plants. At one time it powered an entire sugar beet factory.

In addition there is a sawmill, display of harvest machinery and tractors, a tiny railroad for children and a farmhouse used for wood-stove cooking and foot-powered sewing demonstrations. In June and October the Museum presents old-time threshing bees during which event much of the machinery is in action.

Index

Photo Credits

The following photographs in this book were supplied by outside sources to whom we express our sincere appreciation.

Page 56, Courtesy of the San Diego Wild Animal Park
Page 69, Courtesy of the San Diego Maritime Museum
Page 130, Courtesy of the Museum of Contemporary Art

The adobe ranch house of Juan Jose Warner who was given 44,322 acres of land in 1844 by the Mexican governor. General Kearny passed here in 1846 and the Mormon Battalion in 1847. On October 6, 1858, the Butterfield Stage overnighted at Warner's ranch while making its first 2600-mile, 24-day, run to San Francisco from Tipton, Missouri. The ranch house is located on San Felipe Road about one mile south-east of Highway 79. (***Thomas Page 409, K/8)***

Additional copies of this book and copies of other Explore San Diego books described on the inside covers are available from your area bookstore or from the publisher.

Write to:

Coda Publications
P.O.Bin 711, San Marcos
California, 92079-0711, U.S.A.

Each title is $10, plus $1.50 for shipping.
To this please add the applicable sales tax for your community.
Your personal check is welcome as are postal money orders.